Children
Acting on
Television

Roger Singleton-Turner

A & C Black • London

First published 1999
A & C Black (Publishers) Limited
35 Bedford Row, London WC1R 4JH

ISBN 0-7136-4952-6

A CIP catalogue record for this book is available from the
British Library

Cover photograph by Spike Watson, reproduced by permission
of Arena Images.
Page design by Judith Gordon
Typeset in 10½/12 Adobe Caslon
Printed and bound in Great Britain by
Cromwell Press Ltd, Trowbridge

Contents

Acknowledgements

I would like to thank all of those who filled in questionnaires or who took part in interviews for this book for their thoughts, stories, anecdotes and opinions. Whether or not I have quoted them, they helped confirm experiences that are common to many child actors. It is their words that appear in most of the quotation marks.

Cast List

At the Carlton Junior Television Workshop, Nottingham:
Director of the Workshop   Ian Smith
    Cath Barr, Lauren Richardson,
    Adele McCormack, Andrew Shim,
    Sebastian (Seb) Mahjouri, Jim Tomlinson

At the Italia Conti Academy:
Vice Principal   Mr C. K. Vote
    Cherelle Binns, Nicola Emsley,
    Robert Galas, Caroline Gumm,
    Katie Lucy, Charlotte Moodie,
    George Maguire, Hayley Newton,
    Philip Penny, Daniel Praag,
    Lucas Rush

Child actors from my own productions
    Frances Amey, Tom Brodie,
    Kristy Bruce, Gunnar Cauthery,
    Rachael Goodyer, Tom Szekeres,
    And a special guest appearance of George Armstrong

Tutor-Chaperone
    Lina Wright

From Stagecoach
    Stephanie Manuel

and

From The Anna Scher Theatre
Anna Scher

Also taking part
The Abacus Agency and the Sylvia Young Theatre School in association with Young 'uns Agency

I should also like to thank: Tesni Hollands for giving me time – and the chance to write this book; my wife, Jacqui, and my copy editor Anne Watts for getting the book into its final shape – no mean task; Mary Ann Dudko for information from the USA; Robert Feline for help with rules and regulations; Alison Leon for her help with picture research; Claire Gerschwiler for giving me a schedule I could quote; my daughter for keeping me supplied with coffee and various cats who kept me company whilst I slaved over a hot keyboard. My thanks also go to the BBC for the use of most of the photographs and to Carlton Television for the still from *Welcome to orty-Fou.*

Thank you to the organisations who provided me with information in the course of writing this book: The BRIT School; LIPA; LAMDA; Trinity College of Music, London; The National Association of Youth Theatres; The AES Tring Park School Trust; The Arts Educational School, Chiswick; and Actors' Equity.

Finally, thank you to all the agencies and stage schools up and down the country not mentioned here or in the book who have helped me cast dozens of other splendid children over the years. I have restricted my research to manageable numbers hoping to find a representative cross sample of adults and young actors. This is not a thorough investigation of the whole industry!

ROGER SINGLETON-TURNER 1999

1 *Child Actors*

What is it like to be a child actor?

Well, it's no good asking me – I am only television producer and director – BUT, over the years I have worked on many children's programmes in the UK, from the school-soap *Grange Hill* to *The Demon Headmaster* and *Welcome to orty-Fou*. I have worked with many child actors from different parts of the country, so I can tell you about that, about the auditions, the casting, the agents, and shooting and editing (on film and videotape) with children. I have also sought the views of a lot of child actors to find the range of thoughts and feelings about the experience of acting and its effect on them.

A major part of the book is devoted to the drama training that is available to children. There is a wide range of teaching throughout the country, in part-time classes and at specialist stage schools. The range is so great that I could not visit every organisation – this is definitely not a directory of stage schools and drama clubs. What you will find is a look at the differences between the different types of schools and organisations that you will find in the UK.

There is a section dealing with the law as it currently affects professional performances. You will also find many references to tutors, chaperones and working hours.

In the past, I would have tried hard to discourage any child from wanting to be a professional actor. It is a difficult life – full of rejection, disappointment and waiting. It isn't a 'fair' business; having talent is no guarantee of success. Simply being in the right place at the right time might bring fame and fortune for a while but only those with a huge determination to act will stick the course.

However, the kind of job security people once expected is no longer available in any walk of life. People need entertaining; show business can offer many interesting, reasonably well-paid and skilled jobs. Most of them are quite respectable jobs, too.

A bit of background

My own family had no theatrical connections and my only outlet for 'theatricals' was through puppets. We bought a couple of Pelham (marionette) puppets, and I made a few (very) odd glove puppets. My parents helped me improvise puppet theatres, and I remember building one from Meccano, a popular construction toy in my childhood. My first involvement with putting on a play with a paying audience was at school where I controlled the house tabs. The following year I graduated to Props.

Things have changed a lot since those days. Though lack of money may cause cutbacks in school drama, there are now many more ways of taking part in some kind of drama experience than there were. In the past, being an actor was always regarded as a precarious way of earning a living. It still is. It is quite possible for even a good actor to spend a year or two out of work. On the other hand, some experience of child acting can be helpful if you want to try some of the new jobs in the ever-changing and developing technical areas of television, films and theatre.

My parents did not know about theatre. They were not at all sure about its respectability. My school had a careers master who was fine if you asked about being a teacher or a lawyer, or joining the forces. He knew nothing about television. So I ended up trying to be a doctor. As a medical student, I did learn a lot about 'theatre'. Unfortunately, it was not the kind that doctors need to know about.

Maybe my path into show business would have been smoother if my parents had known more. Maybe they could have encouraged and helped me. On the other hand, I could have ended up with too much help from the typical 'stage mother'. Although the 'stage mother' does exist, I have not had to deal with the worst examples. None of the children I have talked to about this admits to having one. On the contrary: sustained pressure to act, dance or sing appears to come from the child. Since the profession is full of rejection and disappointment, this is just as well. Show business is not kind to those who want to fulfil their dreams through their children.

Throughout my experience of television – I began as a viewer in about 1949, almost before I went to school – Children's Drama has featured children as central characters, the prime movers in the stories. Scriptwriters and programme makers have attempted to tell the story from the child's point of view. Adult dramas have also used children, but that has usually been in the context of children (or childhood) seen from an adult perspective.

My work has been in drama for children. Because of this, most of my projects have featured children. Quite often, the weight of an entire series has rested on the shoulders of one or two children. This is quite a responsibility for them – and for me. Professionally, then, I have ignored the famous dictum: never work with children or animals. Children are a major part of our screen tradition. It is vital that they should be represented as well on screen as any other group. It also seems vital that children should have access to television programmes that are about the world as they see it. A high proportion of these programmes should be from their own culture and in their own language, and they should be shown when children are available to watch. These points are expanded in a document called the Children's Television Charter.

Times have changed; so has the law. In the early days, teenagers often played children's parts. The perspective was usually middle-class; 'political correctness' and 'issues' had not yet been invented. In retrospect many children's programmes were condescending. Adults did talk down to children. But that was what we (as children) expected then. Back in the 1940s and early 1950s, television was for the few – my first viewings were on a neighbour's set. In any case there was only one channel (the BBC) and programmes were shown in black and white. Children's Hour was from 5 p.m. until 6 p.m. and then everything shut down, often until 8 p.m.

Now, a colour tv set is regarded as an essential in almost every home, the digital revolution is upon us and many children are fluent in their use of computers. This was unimaginable fifty years ago. It is difficult to foresee how these changes will affect the appetite for live-action drama, or to guess at the types of drama that may be popular in ten or twenty years time. We hear a lot at the moment about 'non-linear' and 'interactive' forms of drama and other entertainment.* I think there will be a market for such things, but it is likely to be expensive to produce – if there are alternatives within a drama, these must be shot and edited, and this will push costs up significantly.

Increased costs may lead to more work for fewer people. For now, the most popular genres of television remain the 'linear' drama series,

---

* A non-linear or interactive drama might be one where every so often the viewer had the choice of how action moved on, e.g. does the mother divorce the father or not?

whether these are 'soaps', plays or mini-series. We all like a good story and it is inherent in the whole process of storytelling that the storyteller controls the fate of his or her characters. The entertainment lies in the telling and in the twists and turns of plot invented by the storyteller. It has never lain with the audience to choose how the story should end. Would Romeo and Juliet still enthral audiences if the lovers did not die? Would Hamlet be a better play if the Prince of Denmark took wise decisions and acted on them? And so on.

I believe there will be a continuing demand for actors and actresses of all ages to take part in the performances of stories, in whatever medium is likely to be around over the next decades.

Child actors and children

The term 'child actor' in this country includes anyone below the school-leaving age of 16, which can be a few months after the sixteenth birthday. There are restrictions on the working hours and there must be general tuition; pay will consequently be less than for adult actors.

Children's Programmes, however, are made for children up to the age of 11 or 12.

So, for the purposes of this book, if the subject is children-as-an-audience, 'child' means those of 12 or under. If the subject is children-as-actors, then 'child' means those up to – or just over – 16. I would however, not usually refer to the 14–16-year-olds with whom I work as 'children', at least to their faces!

It is important to understand that there are no hard and fast rules for getting on. One person may have started with ballet classes at the age of 3, gone to a stage school, then RADA and never looked back since her first lead in a Jane Austen adaptation. Another individual may make a great hit as an actor at the age of 35, having previously been a taxi-driver.

In acting, starting young is not always an advantage. There was, for example, a successful actor called Bert Parnaby who was a schools' inspector until he retired at the age of 58. He started acting and appeared in many rôles until he died at the age of 75.

The names of child actors that spring to the mind of someone of my age might include Shirley Temple, Jodie Foster, Jack Wild, Dean Stockwell (Quantum Leap), Hayley Mills and Dennis Waterman. Younger readers might think of Nicholas Lyndhurst, Pauline Quirke,

Bonnie Langford and former members of the *Grange Hill* team such as Todd Carty, Susan Tully and others. I have no doubt you could all make your own, much longer, lists.

In fact, there are thousands of child actors – perhaps millions – in this country. Children under 16 who have taken part in any kind of school play, in any drama club production, any youth theatre presentation, any stage school course, any drama on stage, on film or on television, may consider themselves child actors.

The difference between the fourth shepherd at the school round the corner and the leading child in the latest tv drama is perhaps less than you think – and more. It can happen that young children are included in school plays because there is a need in schools not to exclude. It can happen that a child appears who would really rather be elsewhere. Every child I have come across in making television dramas has been there because he or she wanted to be there. It is not unlikely that some of these children have, at some time, played the fourth shepherd. The child who does well and is regularly given good parts in primary school may be nourishing secret dreams of acting professionally. Such dreams are likely to feature working on screen or stage, not in fifteen years' time, but now.

Stage children – the first spark of interest

Any child, from any background, from almost any age may want to act, even without yet understanding what it is all about. Let parents be warned! Children under the age of 3 may already have the performing bug, even when it is not present anywhere else in the family. I write with authority here. I was 'bitten' with the desire to act at the age of 3. It happened through going to seaside shows and listening to radio programmes such as *Mrs Dale's Diary, Dick Barton – Special Agent* and *Journey into Space.* Talking to children over the years, I have found that I was not alone.

One mother writes:

'When [my son] was 2½, he was watching tv and said, "I want to do what those people are doing when I grow up."

'I was slightly concerned, as they were window cleaning. I said, "You want to be a window cleaner?"

'"No," he said. "They are real people pretending. What are they called?"

'"Actors."

'"That's what I want to be," he said.'

Of course, it doesn't always happen like this. It's quite common to find child actors who began dancing, for instance, through watching older sisters in their classes. I have found boys who became interested through elder sisters' activity, but only one girl who followed her brother into acting.

George was 7 when he was taken to see his sister at dancing class. When asked if he wanted to join in, he said, 'No.' The family was actually leaving the class when George changed his mind and went back in. His sister gave it all up. George is now in a full-time stage school.

Charlotte's brother used to do some theatre work and she was taken to watch him. She became interested and is now at full-time stage school. Her brother, like George's sister, has also given up.

It is hard to predict what will set off this desire to perform.

I remember seeing my first pantomime, *Jack and the Beanstalk*, at the Theatre Royal, Nottingham. I suppose I would have been just 5 years old. It was wonderful. There and then, I decided I did not want to be an actor, but to work backstage so I would know how everything worked, especially the flying ballet.

Sebastian saw a pantomime in the same theatre when he was small. That started his interest in acting. Quite a few children have their attention caught simply by seeing a particular show or even a particular film.

Nicola watched a tv programme about ballet and was taken with the desire to dance on point. Katy saw the stage version of *The Wizard of Oz* when she was 6. That was enough for her.

Robert watched tv films and dramas and acted them out at home. This led him to start Saturday dancing classes and he, too, is now at a full-time stage school.

Cath took part in her school production of *Cinderella* and is now hoping for some professional work in television.

Philip had a solo spot in his primary school play. It went well and he loved the applause.

The bug bites, it seems, even without any particular external stimulus. Lauren simply made up plays and stories for herself. Now, she has a number of professional credits to her name.

Few of the children I have cast, and few of those I have spoken to whilst researching this book, have parents in the business – although one boy I met began as a young child with modelling jobs, then joined in his parents' amateur dramatic productions.

Parents

Of course, there are parents who encourage their children and coach them; parents who live through each audition piece, miming their way through each song or monologue.

Although such behaviour is frowned upon – or laughed at – by professional directors and producers, I think it is perhaps understandable. Most parents want to see their children succeed. Many will invest time and money in helping them. Many will become indignant if their child is, in any sense, rejected. Many children find their parents, and their aged reactions, an embarrassment. Parents need the ability to let go a little and to be objective. Children need to allow parents to care.

Most of these remarks could apply equally to young tennis players or ice skaters. There is a fine line between encouragement and pushing too hard. Parents in the USA who spend a fortune on make-up and clothes for their tiny daughters to win 'model' competitions have, too often perhaps, got the balance wrong. It may be great to be a champion at 10, but there is still the rest of your life to live.

Acting is not quite like that. Getting a part does not mean you are the best, because there is no such thing as the best actor. When casting, I go for the person I HAVE SEEN who will fit my production best. Another child whom I have not even shortlisted, may do extremely well for another part, another production, another director. Young actors must become philosophical about this or they cannot survive. 'If you don't get one thing, you might get something else,' was the way one girl put it. Daniel, who is at a full-time stage school, told me the story of a boy who, ' . . . got down to the last two and didn't get the part. He took it so badly [that] he actually left the school.'

The attitude of parents to their children's ambitions will vary. My own were happier about the prospect of my following a 'serious' profession than one in theatre or television. Many parents seem to view acting as a phase their child is going through. Certainly, for the children concerned, going to acting or dancing classes can be something that 'fits the image', something that sounds 'cool'.

There's nothing wrong with that. Acting and dancing classes should help build self-confidence, poise, teamwork, self-esteem, the ability to speak for yourself and so on. Dancing in particular, if it is properly taught, is very good exercise. Any child should gain a lot from such classes. As hobbies go, there is a great deal to be said for drama. It is when a passion develops that there may be a problem.

Ambitions

Around the age of 10, a child may well become engrossed in drama or any number of other activities. For example, many girls take to horses in a big way. They feel that they want to spend the rest of their lives with horses, becoming stable girls, show jumpers, riding instructors and the rest. Time and time again, this passion evolves at about the age of 16 into other kinds of passion, and horses take a back seat, as it were. Now, in some individuals the passion carries on and fuels a determination to fulfil the early ambition. Having this kind of passion does not guarantee success; without it, there is not even the hope of anything like a career. That's horses. The parallel with acting seems apt.

How should parents react? I can tell you that horse riding can consume a great deal of money, and that even the keenest 13-year-olds may regain their sanity by the age of 16, having had some opportunities to explore this world, and get it out of their systems. Acting comes cheaper and is less likely to cause serious injury.

Children who are so passionate about acting that they want to go to a full-time stage school may change their minds later. In many areas, there are now alternatives to this option, and part-time classes may clarify the minds of both parent and child. Such classes are not always cheap but they will certainly cost less than running a horse! In any case, I think it is reasonable to say that a responsible full-time stage school should not accept children unless it feels that there is a natural aptitude present in the first place; that the children have the physique and stamina to do the course, and that they have a DETERMINATION to work in the business.

As Mr Vote, vice-principal of the Italia Conti Academy put it, 'It's a place for "gonna-bees" not "wanna-bees". He would also expect children to have shown commitment by attending part-time dancing or acting classes.

I found the views of some of Mr Vote's pupils interesting. I asked if children should be encouraged to act professionally. There was agreement that the answer was no. 'If they need to be encouraged, they shouldn't be doing it.'

George added, 'Not encouraged to act professionally, but encouraged to act and get trained because if you just get a few big jobs it isn't going to get you far in a career. If it's what you really want to do, you want to train properly. If you come here, you get a professional training.'

Charlotte agreed, 'But I think it should be your choice completely, 101% even if it's just coming to the stage school or working. If you get pushed into it, it's not your true decision, so you're not going to put your heart into it unless it's what you really want.'

It is clearly rather more complicated than that. Children are not necessarily in a position to understand the complications and possibilities of adult life. A 10-year-old put her insight into the problem like this: 'You adults have all been children but we haven't been adults.' Children do change their minds about careers as they get older. It follows that some will regret putting all their eggs in one basket at too early an age. It is hard for parents to find the balance between allowing their children to do – now – what they clearly want to do – now – and being cautious about decisions that may close off other options. How do parents know if they are making the 'right' decisions for their offspring? As Hayley said, 'My dad's in the profession. When I said I wanted to go to stage school, he said, "I didn't mean to push you into it. Are you sure?"'

One boy commented that he'd noticed that some of the parents of younger stage school pupils had seemed pushy.

Lucas remembered a friend who had said he'd wanted to act, so his mother pushed him into training. 'I think that's OK so long as there is a point where he can stop and say, "I think you're being too pushy."'

I asked what they'd say to me if I (as a director) tried to dissuade them from acting. The reaction was summed up by one boy who said, 'If you really want to do it, you'll keep trying.'

They agreed that parents should be facilitators rather than drivers. There was also a sensible comment that parents should also be able to say, 'No,' and stop their children being exploited or stop them from taking part in anything undesirable.

Stage school?

I asked if there was any advice they would have liked when they began at full-time stage school. One response surprised me. 'State school is tougher – people who have been to state secondary school don't take this place for granted. If you do get here, don't take it for granted. Count every second as a moment when you could be learning something. Try to get everything out of every class you go to.'

Most stage schools have, I believe, smaller than average (state school) classes. There should also be an atmosphere of encouragement and mutual support that may not always be present in state schools.

I have heard some stage schools criticised for their attitude to academic work. Certainly, there was one London stage school that used to offer only four academic subjects to its 16-year-old students. That was a long time ago and things there have improved. At Italia Conti's, the attitude to academic work is positive. As one girl said, 'If you go to stage school, don't fall behind in academic work because it's hard to catch up. I got to a point of thinking I didn't need it. I'm still catching up.'

Daniel felt it was important to have some back-up. He gave computer skills as an example. The idea of having something to fall back on did seem fairly widespread among all the children I spoke to. I have certainly come across a few children who reckoned that they worked harder at their stage school than they had in their previous schools. Because the vocational lessons were fulfilling some need, perhaps for self-expression, they were able to tackle normal schoolwork with something approaching enthusiasm. This contrasted with their record of 'bunking off' and other undesirable activity at ordinary schools.

I shall come back to stage schools but, for now, it is important to make it quite clear that many successful child actors never go anywhere near them. There are even directors who seem to feel that stage schools turn out only children who are 'mannered' in their acting and who have little ability. This is unfair. No-one casting children should forget stage schools.

Although it is always advisable to cast your net as wide as time and money allow, on average, I see about forty to fifty children for each main part I cast. If the work is in or near London, there is plenty of choice. Some of the full-time schools have agencies representing children who go to part-time classes. Some agencies represent only children who go to part-time classes. Some agencies run hand-in-hand with their own part-time classes. If we need a child with a regional accent or a child close to a regional location then we would go to the schools of that area looking for local talent. Useful contacts are the local education authority drama (or English) advisers. They will tell us which schools in the area have a strong drama department and we often find young actors in this way.

There are agents and part-time schools in several major British cities but there are few full-time stage schools away from south-east England. There are a growing number of part-time schools run as

Stagecoach (and other) franchises. There are youth theatres of all kinds. In Birmingham, Bristol, Cardiff and Nottingham, there are Children's Television Workshops that were set up by the local Independent Television companies. A casting director could call on any of these when looking for under-16s for any professional job.

Joys and pains

Interestingly, the kinds of story young actors tell about the joys and miseries of acting seem to be common to youngsters with any of these origins. Most of the pains concern rejection. It is all too easy to go to an audition and come away feeling you have done reasonably well – or even very well – only to be told you haven't got the part. The difficulty comes from WANTING the part. If you become interested in the part – or any job for which you are interviewed – you begin to want that job. Indeed, if it is a matter of indifference to you whether you are chosen or not, then it seems unlikely you will come across as the right person for that job. If you become emotionally committed to the idea of the job and are then rejected, there is bound to be some sense of disappointment.

I suppose actors go for more interviews than any other profession. Each must develop a coping mechanism for dealing with rejections. They are bound to happen and it is not simply a matter of talent. There is a great deal of personal preference in casting – especially the casting of children. It finally becomes a matter of which child the director feels will work best in this or that particular part with that particular director. I know I have interviewed children and not even shortlisted them because, however much I liked them, I did not think they were right, or that I could get as good a performance from them as from another child. I have then seen these same children give splendid performances on other projects, with other directors.

I haven't often heard children talk about any substantial job they have done that they didn't enjoy. There are certain odd days of work that are not so enjoyable, and there are days in production where there is boredom or tension. There are also engagements where too little thought has been given to the needs of a child. What walk of life is there without such periods?

What about the joys of acting? If you have the performing 'bug', then the work itself will be, by definition, something you enjoy. Some children talked about the buzz they get from applause. Most talked more in terms of working together with people that, on the whole, they liked. Performing is one of the few ways that children can legally earn money. Because there is a limit on the number of days a child can perform, the sums of money are not likely to be huge – in this country, anyway – but compared with most holiday and Saturday jobs, the pay is good. This can be another satisfaction, although at least one boy, whose name I shall withhold for his own protection, said he would willingly act for nothing! At least, there is always the feeling of pleasure most of us have in completing a job that we know we do well.

I hope you will find this a useful – and even an entertaining – guidebook to acting on television for children. Just remember, what is right for one child is not necessarily right for another. A lifetime in acting is not the best thing for everyone, and the route to success for one may well not work for another. Again, anything you may read here about stage schools, drama schools, agents, production companies, chaperones, tutors or even directors may well differ from your experience.

As someone so famously put it, that's life.

Two warnings and a note

Mention of an organisation in this book should not be taken as a recommendation, any more than an omission should be taken for the reverse.

Anyone who is keen on acting and drama will probably get a lot out of doing it one way or another. If there are affordable facilities that you can get to, why not go for it? However, no children should go to drama classes EXPECTING that they will get parts, fame or money. Lots of children go to part-time schools and never even get close to an audition. Some children do get parts and think they have 'made it'. Some are content with that and move on to other things. Some spend years trying to build an acting career and eventually have to settle for something else; they have wasted time and lost opportunities that could have been fulfilling.

Don't let an unfulfilled dream ruin your life!

You will find cautions like this, and notes about permitted working hours, tuition and so on repeated throughout the book. They are important!

2 *Full-time Stage Schools*

There are so many ways for children to get acting experience that it is difficult to do justice to all the possibilities. There are also several organisations that run examination systems.

There are too many agents, stage schools and others for me to catalogue all of them. What I can do is to give you an idea of the range of things you might find.

Whatever image you may have picked up from shows or tv series such as *Fame* or *The Biz* and from books like *The Swish of the Curtain* and Noel Streatfield's *Ballet Shoes*, you will find the reality is different. For one thing, most training will cost money, sometimes quite a lot of money. There will also be a lot more hard slog than the fiction suggests. In acting, as in everything else, 'genius is one per cent inspiration, ninety-nine per cent perspiration.'*

It pays to shop around for training. Read all the information you can get your hands on and talk to other children and parents. Look carefully at all the options in your area and, if there is an open day, or the equivalent, go and see what goes on.

Full-time stage schools

All stage schools give regular tuition in the National Curriculum core subjects and should be registered with the Department for Education and Employment. The 'academic' teachers should all be properly qualified and registered with the DfEE.

This registration is NOT a seal of approval. However, stage schools like other independent schools can be accredited by the Independent Schools Association, which is linked to the Independent Schools Council. The ISC works to maintain standards among its members and provides a body that can investigate problems and disputes that head teachers and governors cannot sort out. Like most other inde-

*Thomas Alva Edison, inventor.

pendent schools, stage schools charge for their services – only the BRIT School does not. Entry ages vary from school to school. Some take children from 4 years, some start intake at 11.

All stage schools should give instruction in 'vocational' subjects like acting, singing and dancing. You should expect a range of dancing to include tap, modern and ballet, and possible sub-divisions of these categories. The emphasis of the singing lessons often seems to be on a 'show' style rather than on traditional, more operatic techniques.* Acting covers improvisation and working with and preparing a script. Sometimes there might be the chance to learn about stage fighting. There should be some differentiation made between acting on stage and acting for the camera. Tuition in playing a musical instrument should also be available.

Not all pupils will necessarily take all options. Not all the boys take ballet, for instance, but it pays an adult actor to be versatile. No-one is expected to dance like Wayne Sleep, to sing like Dame Kiri Te Kanawe AND to act like Kenneth Branagh, but an actor should move reasonably gracefully in a dance sequence and be able to sing, or at least deliver a number. Dame Judi Dench told me she would not describe herself as a singer, yet she was in the London production of *A Little Night Music* and played the lead in *Cabaret*. She was also one of the leads in a musical version of *Comedy of Errors* by the Royal Shakespeare Company that won the title Best Musical of 1976. Perfect and precision singing is not always necessary.

It is harder to think of examples of actors not renowned for dancing. There was a story about Clark Gable in *Gone with the Wind*. There is a ballroom sequence in that film where he had to dance with his leading lady whilst the camera followed the couple around the room. According to the tale, Mr Gable stood on a low trolley that was wheeled around so that he did not have to move his feet at all. With my dancing ability, I think similar trickery would be needed for me!

Meanwhile, back at the stage school, the system of timetabling will vary a great deal. One school may integrate vocational classes with academic subjects so that pupils move from maths to tap then to history in the course of a morning. Other schools may have pupils working academically in the mornings and in vocational classes in the afternoons. Another timetable might concentrate the academic work

---

*If 'classical' singing is the main interest, there are specialist music schools, junior departments in the major music colleges and private music teachers.

into three days of the week and allow two full days for the other classes. Each school arrives at its own conclusions of what works best for its particular circumstances.

Most schools will put on their own productions each year. Some have a stage of their own; others may hire a theatre. The policy for such shows is usually to involve as many of the pupils as possible. Sometimes directors and casting directors may be invited to such performances.

Of the stage schools I have visited, it is notable how much their facilities vary. One school uses the premises of a Baptist church – although there is no religious link, so far as I am aware. Another uses an old school building. A third took over what looks like an office block in the City of London. None of these has its own sports facilities – but then this is often true for other types of school, too, and some stage schools do have enough land for sports. In any case, there should be no lack of physical activity. Arguably, dance is as physically demanding in terms of co-ordination, strength and stamina as most sports.

I have not enquired very deeply into the financial status of any particular stage school. In order to survive, however, they all have to succeed as businesses. They all charge fees as do other private schools. Those which have boarding facilities obviously also charge for them. Most have agencies working with the school, but there is little leeway for the agency's profit to subsidise the school. One or two schools are able to offer a small number of bursaries or scholarships in exceptional circumstances.

Stage schools usually have licensed chaperones available to look after children at auditions or while they are working professionally. In the course of an actual engagement, the chaperones will be paid by the television Production Company, although their duty is always to look after the interests of the child.

Schools specialising in the arts

For those who have a great interest in theatre, but who may feel that neither the part-time schools nor the full-time stage schools are appropriate, there are alternatives. For example, the Arts Educational Trusts are different. Founded at the same time as the Italia Conti Academy, there are now two schools, run quite separately. The Arts Educational Tring Park School Trust, Buckinghamshire, is a boarding school and the other, in Chiswick, London, is not.

A singing lesson at the Italia Conti Academy

In essence, they are both private schools where pupils are generally discouraged from taking time out to perform professionally. They both offer general education and training in dance, drama and musical theatre, seeking to develop confidence and poise rather than to produce child performers. Entrance is by audition as well as academic test and prospective pupils may be asked to dance, sing or recite a poem. To a greater or lesser extent, dance and related activities replace sport on the curriculum.

Although juniors are discouraged from taking part in most kinds of professional work, some from the Chiswick school do appear in English National Opera and Ballet productions. Some juniors do go on to become professional actors, but many pursue other careers. At the Chiswick school there are also foundation courses leading to 'A' levels for 16-year-olds and a full-time drama school for students of 18 and over, offering a course leading to a degree in drama. The Tring school has a thriving sixth form with students going on to study Performing Arts and many other university courses.

Schools like these may be more appropriate for some readers of this book than some of the other options.

The BRIT School for Performing Arts and Technology . . .

. . . is based in Croydon, to the south of London, and is unique in being funded by the Department for Education and Employment (DfEE), major record companies and other industrial sponsors. There are no fees. The school has entries at 14 and 16. Up to 16 students are expected to follow the National Curriculum. After 16, they take a variety of vocational courses in dance, music, drama and musical theatre. Subjects include production and music technology. All students are encouraged to do IT courses. The view is that as few as five per cent of students will be able to build a full-time career as performers, and IT gives some useful back-up.

Students are required to live within an hour's travel of the school and there are no boarding facilities. Lodgings are available locally, sometimes in the homes of other students.

The school is unusual in having five terms of eight weeks each.

The emphasis here is on performance rather than on academic work, so qualifications may be GNVQs or 'A' levels. Interestingly, the school makes a point of its support for students with dyslexia.

There are two open evenings a year, usually in October and January. Selection is by interview and group workshops with several candidates. Applicants are expected to show a level of commitment and evidence of interest in the performing arts and/or the associated business, media and technological aspects.

As the funding for the school comes from the BRIT Awards and the record industry, there is, unsurprisingly, a bias towards music courses.

The Liverpool Institute for Performing Arts . . .

. . . was founded through the efforts of Paul McCartney in his old school building. Other patrons include Richard Branson who is also a sponsor for the BRIT school. The courses here are geared towards degrees and diplomas, so it is really for those aged 18 and over. I include it here because I have heard people mention it as a place similar to the BRIT School. Quite clearly, this is misleading. But now you know!

Attitudes to stage schools

As I have said, some people in television regard the full-time stage schools with some suspicion. On the other hand, their students should have a basic familiarity with such concepts as reading a script, improvising and working as a group.

However, it is sometimes felt that full-time stage schools restrict the options of their pupils by giving, too early, too specialised an education.

I would not want anyone reading this book to feel that I am advocating any particular school, system or route into acting. What is right for one child may be disastrous for another. Though restricting educational options is not a good idea, some find the more supportive smaller, stage schools helpful – especially to a child who marches to the beat of a different drum.

However, simply attending your local school may be the best option for some. There are state schools with strong drama and music departments. The Intake High School in Leeds is one such. Quite a few of its pupils have found work in television, both for Yorkshire Television and for the BBC.

Finance

In addition to fees, students may be expected to buy some kind of 'uniform', even if this is only a sweatshirt. Dance classes will need appropriate footwear. Most children hate to be different and hate being left out, so you may have to spend money on special clothing. Quite often, there is a second-hand trade in some items such as tap shoes.

Some schools offer additional lessons for additional fees. There may be other activities that need money spent on them. These could range from Summer Schools to costumes for a particular production. If the school you are interested in is a long way from home, then boarding or other lodging may be needed. This is not cheap. Travel to and from auditions can become expensive, and you may have to pay for a chaperone.

Earning money and Local Authorities

Children do not get large fees for their work. They can only perform on 20, 40 or 80 days in a year. They can legally work only for a maximum of three and a half hours a day. They must have tutors and chaperones. Often, they end up with private cars driving them around. They tend to have less 'flexibility' in acting terms than adults. These are all factors children tend to forget when they complain about their rates being lower than those for adults.

The local authority has the power to ensure that a proportion of a child's earnings is banked. After all the expenses are removed, there is not likely to be enough money to pay for school fees or other major expenses. It seems wrong and exploitative to me to expect children to earn money for their families but some parents do expect it. Some parents also expect to chaperone their own children on all occasions. Since chaperones are paid, this can become a form of exploitation, too.

That said, it beats newspaper rounds for money and young actors are able to use their earnings in constructive ways. One girl was able to buy herself a cello after one job and a piano after another. In a way, she was ploughing her earnings back into her education to buy herself better facilities than her parents could have afforded on their own. This seems both reasonable and useful.

It pays to shop around.

3 *Part-time Schools*

Part-time schools are organisations teaching drama or dance to young people outside regular school hours.

Many girls and a few boys attend dancing classes. They have been around in most parts of the country for many years. Quite often, they will take children from the age of 3 and upwards. Very young children want to dance without knowing anything of classes; it is usually parents who look for them and examine their reputations.

Ballet, tap and modern dance are widely available and standardised examinations will be on offer. There will be parents' events where you can go and watch your offspring perform and possibly more elaborate shows, on a proper stage. Some of these schools will provide a junior *corps de ballet* for local pantomimes, both amateur and professional. Teaching standards and facilities will vary enormously from one school to another – although the fact that there are external standards for the examinations does give some means of comparison.

Drama classes also vary in purpose, teaching methods and facilities.

The Anna Scher Theatre

The Anna Scher Theatre draws its students from Islington. It is unlike anything else I have seen. It is probably the best known of all the part-time schools and has had a far-reaching influence on children's drama. Anna Scher drives the phenomenon herself. There are no Anna Scher franchises. There is only one Anna Scher.

'The Anna Scher Theatre has one thousand members and a waiting list of three thousand five hundred. Improvisation is the staple, combining community spirit with professionalism. AST's method is about addressing conflict resolution through effective communication skills, rôle reversal, olive branching, notice compliments and the pebble in the pond philosophy.'

There are classes for children from 6 years old and for adults and professionals. There are also a Summer School in August and short courses and educational visits 'for teachers, students, social workers, actors and anyone interested in AST's Method'.

The school has a successful agency but ' . . . children under 16 do not do modelling or advertising for commercial products. All management profits go to the Theatre for the benefit of all the members who are kept grounded, focused and in touch with reality.'

Anna keeps the costs as low as possible for each child. They pay session by session. They are not expected to buy any particular item of kit – such as sweatshirts. The agency tries to make Production Companies pay for chaperones, for auditions and for fares – not always successfully. If children do have to pay for a chaperone, where a parent is not available, then the cost is split between all the children attending the particular session. (Once into production, it is nearly always the company that will pay the chaperone.)

The AST has only a single-page entry in Children's and Young Performers' Spotlight, showing a group of young actors. If casting directors need individual photographs, they can telephone to request them. The child's family is responsible for supplying these. In practice, directors will often observe a session with the right age group, watch the warm-up and then select students for interview from those present. 'It is much more sensible for one person to come across London than for twelve children to go across to you.'

Some people think you have to be beautiful to act. Anna would not agree. 'Everybody is welcomed . . . and we work on the talent – it's all about developing talent to a high professional standard.' The classes are child orientated and stage-struck parents are not encouraged.

The credits are impressive. The AST is ' . . . known for producing actors like Pauline Quirke, Linda Robson, Kathy Burke, Frances Amey [she played Dinah for me in *The Demon Headmaster*], Phil Daniels and Ray and Mark Burdis.' How do they do it? Anna believes talent is the key.

Values

I asked Anna if she took people purely on a 'first come, first served' principle. She told me she did, so I asked if there was any sense in which she looked for talent. I found her answer interesting. She said she believed everyone had talent but tenacity was the key to success.

Anna is unusual because her drama teaching goes hand in hand with the teaching of a moral sense. She encourages her students to be responsible and to respect one another. She emphasises the importance of conscience and of acknowledging the difference between right and wrong.

Stars – or not

It is significant that Anna feels very strongly that we should not use the term 'child star'. She compares child actors with child swimmers and child tennis players, and says the use of the word 'star' makes them lose touch with reality.

Who the school is for

I asked whom the school was for. 'My name is associated with children and young people but, in fact, I have as many adults as children …We want people to come because they enjoy drama. It's very much a community theatre. I take them in at 6 and at 66 they're still here …'

National Association of Youth Theatres

There are many Youth Theatres up and down the country. You can find the National Association of Youth Theatres' address at the back of the book. The Association ' . . . is an umbrella organisation which supports and develops the work of youth theatres nationally. Its aim is to increase the range and quality of youth theatre in the UK by generating public support at national and local levels.

'There are an estimated seven hundred youth theatres in the UK involving sixty thousand young people of many different ages and backgrounds. All anybody needs to join are interest and enthusiasm; you can learn skills that will be helpful in many other fields of work or play and have a great time while doing so. Membership is available to anyone from 5 to 25.'

Activities vary and may involve workshops developing skills in improvisation, scripted work, lighting, set design, music, mime, dance, costume and writing.

The organisation has a database of theatre groups; so, if you write to them with a self-addressed envelope, they can put you in touch with your nearest groups. A report on theatres in the Association says that, '77% of young people travel less than 5 miles to their YT.'

The Association issues a regular bulletin to its members and twice-yearly publications for Youth Theatre members and for Youth Theatre workers. There is also an annual camp where young people from all over the country can gather for theatrical activities.

Funding is a perennial problem. Many local authorities offer some support. Some are withdrawing or cutting this funding. Part of the work of the Association is the co-ordination of representation at high level to fight cuts and to find new funding. Each group works independently, so methods of raising funds will vary, but there is usually an annual subscription. This is kept as low as possible.

There are many actors who quote experience with Youth Theatre as part of their backgrounds. Among them are Robson Green who became famous following his appearances in *Soldier, Soldier*, and Matt Savage, who played Garth in *Birds of a Feather* for seven years. On the whole, youth theatres are not set up to work as agents for their actors, so tv people are less likely to approach them than some of the other kinds of organisation in this chapter. That said, if we wanted local young people for a particular project, or someone with a precise regional accent, then we could approach any youth theatre in the appropriate area. The emphasis is certainly on drama and not sweetie commercials!

The facilities available to any particular group and the range of its activities will vary from those of its neighbours. Training has been available to part-time youth theatre workers for some time now and it is seen as important to the future of the movement. It is up to you to check out your local group and see whether you suit each other.

Stagecoach

Stagecoach is probably the largest single part-time stage school organisation in the UK. It has also claimed to be the best. I think some other part-time schools might dispute that!

It all began with Stephanie Manuel trying to fill what she saw as a gap in the market. 'Having had a child of my own who was very keen on the performing arts, being married to an actor and being involved myself, I looked around for somewhere where my little boy could learn the three disciplines of the performing arts: dance, drama and singing.' She was disappointed. 'So, when the time was right I got a friend of mine interested in the idea … And together we started it, way back in 1988.'

Stephanie's idea caught on and there are now Stagecoach franchises throughout Great Britain. There are also franchises in Malta, Eire and the USA.

Stagecoach is not just for aspiring actors. It is non-selective. Each school has its own principal and a maximum of forty-five students. There are three hours of teaching a week for each group divided into: one hour of jazz and modern dance, one hour of drama and one hour of singing. Experienced professionals teach in all the schools and, as the children are split into three age groups, no class has more than fifteen students. Stagecoach inspects each school regularly to ensure 'quality control'.

Many children are represented by the school's own agency and some do land rôles in professional theatre or tv productions. There is a Stagecoach National Showcase Production every year in London and a magazine for young performers called Mask.

How it operates

Stagecoach asks you to book for a term at a time, but you can pay for a couple of trial lessons before you commit yourself. Although the fees sound high, when you work it out at an hourly rate over the thirteen-week term at three hours a week, the costs do compare favourably with other kinds of class. Additional costs include the Stagecoach sweatshirts and appropriate dance shoes. Some schools are able to help one or two students financially, and there are discounts for other family members. There was one family with five children who were all members!

The publicity says, 'If you're looking for a place to polish your stage skills and enjoy yourself while you do it, then your local Stagecoach school is for you. You gain poise, confidence, self-esteem, speak and move better, and express yourself more easily … If you're aged between 6 and 16, you're welcome.'

Classes often take place on school premises, after school or at weekends. From the demonstration class I watched in Darlington, I would say that the publicity is fair. The ability was obviously very mixed, but there was a good atmosphere, with teachers who were imaginative and enthusiastic.

Stephanie told me that, although ten years ago there were only five schools, ' … from those, a number of young people have gone into the business and are being about as successful as the average youngster going into the business ... Mostly full of talent and not particularly full of work. But it is the way of things.'

Stephanie's advice

I asked her what advice she would give anyone who wanted to be an actor. 'Don't!' she laughed. 'We try very hard to bring the children up to realise the difficulties and disappointments that the acting profession affords. We do that in rather a practical way by having this huge agency and putting anybody who asks on the agency's books. It's central to our ethos that we don't pick children for their talent. Stage schools do. It's right for them but for us it isn't. So they get to learn from quite an early age about the disappointments involved in casting procedures and conditions, and how close you can get and still not get the job.

'Part of the education that we give children is to make them aware of the horrors of the theatrical profession. And if they go through eight or nine years of Stagecoach, as some of them do, and still want to act, then I think you've got to be able to say, "Good for you, then. Go for it!"

'The other thing I always recommend wherever possible ... is that they do a university degree first ... to fall back on if their ambition for the theatre should fail them.'

Knowing what Anna Scher thinks about the term 'child stars', I asked Stephanie for her view. She thought the term something of a misnomer in view of the large number of capable child actors.

I asked her about the benefits of theatrical training. She said, 'The children will show you the benefits. A child will come along perhaps afraid to move away from the wall ... After two or three terms, you happen to notice what's going on. Suddenly, this child is in the centre of the row. That's the tingle factor. That's the thing that makes you realise that what we're doing is immensely valuable.'

She added that if parents fall on hard times, this is the kind of child she would encourage her principals to help. 'If you see something that's really doing a child good – that's the way we measure it; it's watching them grow as people.'

There is now at least one other organisation offering similar facilities.

Junior Television Workshops

In the early 1980s, some of the Independent Television Companies set up Junior Television Workshops. ITV franchises have changed hands, companies have merged or altered, but the Workshops carry on. They vary, particularly in the matter of funding, but all have some things in common. There are Workshops in Bristol, Cardiff and Birmingham, but I chose to visit the first, the Carlton (Central) Junior Television Workshop in Nottingham. This workshop has a catchment area of about thirty miles; any student who can arrive there by 5 p.m. will be considered for a place.

It was founded by Lewis Rudd MBE in 1983. Ten years later, he wrote, 'One of my main concerns when I joined Central in 1981 was that our children's and young people's programmes should reflect the area in which the company was based, particularly in the field of young actors.

'Rather than scour every school in the Midlands, I decided on a completely new idea: an out-of-school drama workshop in Nottingham, funded by Central. I asked Peter Murphy, a television producer with a background of working in Theatre in Education, to set it up. Sue Nott, who had experience both in professional theatre and teaching, became the Workshop's first leader . . .

'The first priority was to find children to take part as actors in programmes, but I also realised that the Workshop would provide us with a panel of consultants to assess programmes and try out ideas.

'The Workshop started with children in the 11–15 age group, which I considered to be the most useful for casting purposes. It soon became clear that a younger group would also be an advantage, particularly because many children's programmes are aimed at younger audiences. The over-16 group was a natural development, as the first generation of children became older. It was equally inevitable that we should set up a parallel group in Birmingham.'

Central Television is now owned by Carlton Television and the Workshops continue to flourish, now under the guidance of Ian Smith in Nottingham and Colin Edwards in Birmingham. Students appear in a wide range of stage and television productions, in local theatres and in the Workshops' own productions. Television productions may well be for companies other than Carlton – even for the BBC!

Because of the way the Workshops are funded, it is unnecessary for the Workshop to take an agent's commission. This is most unusual.

The fact is that the Workshops are a great resource for the company, but there is more. Ian Smith said, 'I think Carlton are quite sensitive to their responsibilities to the region, considering that it's a London organisation …

'The fact is that we continue to contribute very strongly, not just in casting but in workshopping ideas … through a lot of award-winning programmes. We have produced award-winning directors from the Workshops. There are writers out there. There are people producing … Ultimately, I suppose what we're looking at is a saving in terms of the trawl one would have to make around schools.'

Getting in

I asked him how children were selected.

'We go through two stages. There are 60 kids in our [11 to 16] group. For that group, we audition [in the Spring around 600 kids …] from the top Juniors for entry in September at 11 up to 14. We stop at 14 because we feel that, if we take them on at 15, they're coming into the group in their final year of GCSEs, which, we've found, is not a good idea.

'That 11 to 16 group is auditioned. It's billed as an audition, so they know they're coming along and they're going to be tested in that sort of a way. Each audition lasts two-and-a-half hours and we have our older kids helping us … They set up various improvisations with them and go in and act on that. The aim, really, is just to get the kids relaxing and having fun. At the end of the day, they go out having had a good experience. This is really very important.

'From that 600 we'd have a shortlist of about 60. And that shortlist is usually about three hours long. We send out a script – and do a little bit of script, just to get a feeling of how they work more formally.'

Ian's next comment ties in very well with my own experience when casting for productions: 'We HAVE taken kids who have done extremely well on the improvisation and less well on the script. Increasingly the script is important … Occasionally, you take a flyer on a kid you know has had bad help from his parents or has never really done any script-work before and he's misunderstood, maybe, what you're expecting of it: he's doing it in panto style when it's screaming out to be naturalistic. Those sorts of things you can work on and adjust.'

The under-11 audition is more of a series of open drama workshops taking place over the Whitsun half-term. The exercises usually take the form of improvisations with one of the 11 to 16 group.

I asked about other ways of joining. 'If parents push and say they know we've got a main group and "How do they get in?" then, obviously, I'll be looking out for potential talent. If there are spaces in a group, then we will invite them in.'

His ideal is that the letter saying the Workshop wants to take on a particular child should come as a 'rather nice surprise', as a follow-up to the fun day of the workshop-audition.

For both age groups '… we really try and get the idea that it's a one-off experience.'

Amateur theatre

Some 'professionals' have used the word 'amateur' insultingly over the years. This is unfair. Amateur actors act because they love acting. That is what 'amateur' means. Many people do not wish to be professional actors. This does not mean they do not have acting talent, experience or ability. The standard of the amateur groups is very variable, but some undoubtedly put on excellent shows. Some groups, especially the larger ones with more frequent productions, may have space and opportunities for young people.

Many schools still have the chance to put on school plays. In fact, the first productions I worked on, backstage, were at school. Some universities have very strong theatre groups. Oxford and Cambridge have turned out many successful professional actors, yet these groups are 'amateur'. As a student, I worked on many amateur productions. Some had professional producers and designers. One of my fellow students said something I have always remembered: 'Being professional isn't a matter of being paid, it's an attitude of mind.'

Good amateur experience can help you explore some of the possibilities of drama and give you a clearer idea of whether you want to try to make the move into the professional world.

Disabilities

I must write something about this even though I do so from a position of relative ignorance. I am aware that on-screen representation of different kinds of disability groups is lamentable. I have tried to find actors with disabilities more than once and have failed. It does no-one any service to cast any disabled children just because they are disabled. A strong acting ability is essential, so is stamina. If a part has not been written for a specific disabled child or at least with a specific disability in mind, casting becomes very difficult.

It is all the harder because there are few drama classes available to both able-bodied and disabled people, the best known probably being The Chicken Shed in North London. Graeae (pronounced 'grey-eye') is a theatre group in North London that does offer full facilities to disabled actors, but it deals mainly with adults.

A small (but increasing) percentage of the members of the youth theatres have disabilities of various sorts. The National Association of Youth Theatres can put you in touch with groups in your area. Around 80% of youth theatres have an open membership policy, allowing entry to anyone who wishes to participate.

The remainder do use entry auditions, but these are 'a device to control numbers when the YT is over-subscribed and/or to ensure that the young people can demonstrate a sufficient level of ability to operate effectively within the group.'

Apart from problems of perceptions and understanding among us in the Business there are two main areas of difficulty.

- The first is the nature of most kinds of traditional dance and drama. There are strength and stamina considerations. Physique is a major consideration in selecting any mainstream dance students and there are stories of the major ballet schools rejecting dancers who are merely too tall, too short or who develop the 'wrong' proportions.
- The second is the mundane problem of premises.

Anna Scher says of her own building, 'This theatre is open to everyone but it would have to be razed to the ground in order to have what RADA has. And it's cost RADA £30 something million to completely transform its building. But I've had disabled people. If people feel they can work round what we have got, great.'

This is not ideal, but it is a case of working with what you have in the realms of what is possible NOW. The cost of modifying the Anna Scher Theatre to accommodate wheelchairs would run into hundreds of thousands of pounds that are just not available – even the Lottery would not help.

There is a similar problem at the Junior Television Workshop in Nottingham. It has a lease on two reasonably large rooms in an old basement in the city centre. Conversion would be extremely expensive, and against the terms of the lease. Part of the problem here is that Carlton Television holds its franchises for five-year terms. The company cannot afford an investment that might disappear if the franchise went elsewhere next time round.

There is a willingness to look at the issue and to move forward. There ARE too-rare successes and exceptions. There are also brick walls to break through.

I am sorry I cannot be more positive

Child actors – retiring early

A number of children do just one professional project. They do it successfully, but then find, perhaps, that their time becomes consumed by other interests – or schoolwork. Many stop around GCSEs or when they move on to Higher Education. For these – and even for those burning to become adult actors, the part-time schools have much to offer.

4 Agents, Photographs, Publications, Equity and Examinations

There are dozens of theatrical agents representing the thousands of adult actors up and down the country. Most are concentrated in London and, of those, most are in the West End. Since a lot of the business is done by phone, fax, post and even e-mail, the location now is less important than it used to be. A small proportion of these agents represent children, usually only one or two per agency. Most children who have agents are represented by specialists, who have formal or informal links with their stage schools or through their part-time schools.

Agents will try to find work for their clients; they arrange auditions and organise chaperones; they negotiate contracts; and they smooth out disputes and offer advice to their clients. They can also arrange for photographs to be taken that may appear in *Children's and Young Performers' Spotlight*. (*Spotlight* is the main actors' directory in the UK. Several volumes cover a variety of categories as well as actors and actresses.)

All the agencies, except, perhaps, the Junior Television Workshops, take a proportion of any payment for professional work. 10–12.5% seems reasonable. Anything over 15% is getting steep in my view, but it does depend on what kind of service you are getting from the agent.

When looking for an agent – or any kind of training – do not be afraid to ask questions. Do ask to see any pamphlets, leaflets or brochures and do make sure you know what costs you may be letting yourself in for. A good tip is to try and talk to other clients.

Going it alone?

It is perfectly possible for an individual to place a picture in *Spotlight* with a contact telephone number. But this is one of the few options I would say is almost always a bad idea – certainly where a child is concerned. I believe the child and the parents need a buffer between them and the Production Company and vice versa. It is even harder to telephone a child's home and make tentative enquiries that will probably not be followed up than it is to make these same enquiries of an adult actor. It is much easier to talk to an agent who is well used to dealing with general enquiries.

What the Production Company wants

When a Production is looking for children, whether it needs one child or a hundred, it will become known on the 'grapevine'. The Production will also, probably, send out a breakdown. The agent will respond to this information, however it is obtained, by supplying the Production with a list of appropriate children and asking for them to be included in the audition. The list should include all children with enough available days, who are of the right sex, age, height, or ethnic background, having an appropriate accent, and the requisite talent.

Sometimes we will receive a list running into dozens from one agent and maybe two or three suggestions from another. I have found I am as likely to choose from the smaller list as from the larger because some thoughtful pre-selection on the part of the agent may be very helpful.

The agent is in a good position to know the 'going rate' for a particular type of job with a particular company, and will negotiate as far up the range as possible. Secondary matters like hotel accommodation, fares or transport to location and problems with family holidays might all come into the discussions. Odd days of non-availability for, for instance, an important school event, SATS or GCSEs should also be sorted out at this stage. The agent may also help with licensing.

Because the rules of work change as children get older, it is important for those involved in casting to know their exact ages. This is partly to do with the maximum number of days we can expect to have the children available and partly because mixing children of different ages in a group where all are supposed to be of one age it does not seem to work – even if the heights are identical.

I believe that the agents outside London, mainly representing local children, will be asked most often to provide children for productions of nearby companies. There will also be demand from distant production companies needing children with particular local accents or London companies shooting on regional locations.

Sylvia Young runs both the Young 'uns Agency and the Sylvia Young Theatre School. The agency represents children from all over the country who do not go to the school, as well as the full-time pupils. The Italia Conti Academy runs satellite schools, and the agency represents full-time pupils from these as well as from the Academy. (The Arts Educational School at Chiswick also runs satellite schools, but they discourage professional engagements in term time and do not count themselves as an agency.) Probably the largest client base is to be found in Stagecoach.

Travel is significant for many would-be child actors. Directors or casting directors quite frequently do the rounds of local stage schools although some may show marked preferences in their choice of the places they visit regularly. If I feel I am likely to see a dozen or more young hopefuls in one place, then I am willing to travel some distance to audition them.

If an agency has only one or two children whom it considers right, or does not have a centre convenient for most of their young clients, then I might arrange for such children to come to me. I have had individuals travelling from Devon and from Tyneside. My productions could not afford to pay for these trips: it was the parents' decision as to whether they wished to speculate on their child getting a part. It just is not possible for casting directors to interview all possible children for the first time on their home territory. This means that children who live some way away from the major centres of production are likely to have either fewer opportunities for auditions or much higher travelling expenses. As the business works now, I do not see a simple way round these problems.

What an agent can provide

On the whole, if you are serious about acting, it should be helpful to have an agent. It is a business relationship and any deal done with an agent needs just the same kind of care as any other business arrangement. The benefits of having a good agent are considerable:

- agents are in a position to know what work is available for any particular client;
- they will negotiate the best possible terms;

- the Production Company can telephone an agent and enquire about the availability of a child without arousing false hopes or expectations;
- the Production can ask detailed questions about experience and ability and expect a moderately objective answer;
- the agent should be able to advise on matters of licensing.

It is essential to look around and get as much information as possible. No agent is obliged to take you on, but then you are not obliged to join a particular agent. If you have doubts, keep on looking. You are setting up a two-way business relationship, so you need to feel confidence in the agent. Conversely, the agent should be able to trust you to keep the agency informed of things like family holidays, compulsory school trips and public examinations.

The agent also needs to know if there is health problem or injury that may affect a booking. On the whole, the children I have met have tended not to hold strong 'orthodox' religious views, but if there are matters of religious (or other) diet, Sabbath restrictions or dress codes, then the agent needs to be aware of these things before auditions take place. (I guess it is unusual, but I did cast a girl who was allowed to wear only shalwar kameez. There was a trainee director I met, too, who had to leave the studios before sunset once a week.)

An agent's point of view

A few agents, like Abacus, take on children who have no particular connections with any stage school. Children, or their parents, find Abacus through word-of-mouth contact. For instance, a boy got a major part in *Cider with Rosie*; the other children in the cast live in Gloucestershire and asked him who his agent was. Abacus, run by Sue Scarrett in Middlesex, now has a knot of children in Gloucestershire; the agency has taken on other children on the recommendation of drama teachers.

I asked Sue what she had to say about children acting. Success, she told me, comes from parents who enjoy the whole involvement in drama. It is not enough just to go to singing and dancing lessons after school. 'You have to take every opportunity,' she says. This can mean being prepared to bring a child to London from Weston-super-Mare, Gloucestershire or further afield for an audition. It is an expensive business for parent and child both in time and travel.

Life can be frustrating for the agent who specialises in representing children. Sometimes, a young actor has difficulty in finding an agent, and is taken on as a teenager by a 'child agent' – and will be grateful for finally getting representation. As soon as such teenagers find work, they may move on to a more prestigious agent, having used the 'child agent' simply to get themselves launched. People do change agents for all kinds of reason, but this behaviour is exploitative. Agents have feelings, too!

British Actors' Equity ...

... is the union for actors. It represents adult actors and other performers (over the age of 16), directors, designers and the like. There is also a student membership system for people on a large number of full-time courses that have accreditation from the National Council for Drama Training (NCDT). The courses on the scheme are reckoned to be the equivalent of professional experience, so transfer to full membership follows easily when there is an offer of a full professional contract.

Equity works to ensure that managements throughout all branches of show business employ members on fair contracts. All actors benefit from Equity's work. It runs a regular newsletter and can offer information and advice on all kinds of topics. It does not work as an agency and does not find work for actors.

In addition to adult and student memberships, young actors from 14 to 16 years of age can join as Equity Youth Members. For this, it is necessary to have a contract for professional work for which the pay is at least half the adult rate. There are thousands of adult members in the UK, but only a hundred or so Youth Members.

Anyone seriously considering becoming a professional actor should most certainly consider membership.

Spotlight, Contacts and *The Stage*

Spotlight runs to eight basic volumes with supplements for various special groups. Some local libraries have copies in their reference section. There are also CD-ROM versions available. The same company annually publishes *Contacts*, which lists all kinds of organisations from agents to vehicles and transport. Unfortunately, no trade directory is totally up to date and totally comprehensive, but

Contacts does provide a lot of addresses fairly economically.

There are twenty-nine agencies and stage schools listed in my current edition of the *Children's and Young Performers' Spotlight*.

Another useful source of information about what is going on in the world of acting is the *Stage* newspaper, which is published each week and is not mentioned elsewhere in this book.

Photographs

You will be expected to provide decent-quality pictures for any agency – those over 16 may need to send off a lot of photographs to agents merely to find one willing to represent them. For children, the photographs can usually be organised through the agency but they can be costly. The Sylvia Young Agency issues a general advice sheet to would-be actors, which has this to say about photographs, 'Preferably, the photo should be a professional black and white RECENT head shot. Get a good photo – reproduced inexpensively.' There are lists of 'copying and duplicating services' in local Yellow Pages.

Whether the object is to find an agent or to find a part, some photographs may not be returned for some time; some may not be returned at all. Do keep both negatives and original prints. Send a copy print. Many b & w copying processes work from a print.

Many agents have their own directories of clients, with photographs. Usually, these are glossy brochures sent out free to possible employers. Sometimes, the agent prefers to send only the photos of specific children. Both systems have their advantages. Many agents have a preferred style, which means using an experienced photographer. A number of prints will probably be needed – one, perhaps, for *Spotlight*, one for the agent's brochure and several to be available for sending out to casting directors. Some of the smaller agents use any photographs they are given, taken anyhow by anybody. One agent even sent me a roughly cut-out half-photograph. I know photography is an expensive business and it can be hard for some families, but that particular agent did not impress me favourably.

The other problem with photographs of children is that they do not grow up with their subjects. Children change rapidly in look from year to year; there is often a time lag between a photograph being taken and its appearing in an agency's directory or *Spotlight*. Both kinds of directory are issued annually, and casting directors don't always have the most up-to-date version. It is easy to think a child looks possible in a picture, only to find a totally unrecognisable person turning up to audition. A few months can make a huge difference in height, and the appearance of some girls can go from 'child' to 'late teenager' in a year. It is important to include the date of birth with the picture.

There are photographers who specialise in 'theatrical' photographs. It is not quite the same as High Street portrait photography. Take advice on this from the agency and arrange a chaperone. Taking photographs of children needs the right kind of approach.

Exams

It is, of course, possible to take various combinations of drama, English, music and theatre studies at GCSE and 'A' level. It is also possible to take other kinds of examination: I have long been aware of the LAMDA (London Academy of Music and Dramatic Art) examinations, where it is possible to work through the grades in various aspects of speaking and acting starting as young as 4-years-old. Trinity College London has also developed a system of examinations for people from 5-years-old to advanced postgraduate levels. The syllabus of the Guildhall School of Music and Drama is similar to that of LAMDA

LAMDA has, perhaps, concentrated on the UK and on speech and drama. Trinity College has, in the past, concentrated more on overseas students for speech, although its music exams are well known in the UK – especially in this household. Since 1999, this has changed. They have developed an entirely new syllabus that looks at music and speech as part of Performance Arts. It is possible to approach these exams on your own, as part of a group or in pairs. Though there is an emphasis on music and musical theatre, it is not necessary to take music as part of any given exam. Further Education Colleges are receiving funding for grades 5 and higher, and grades 6, 7 or 8 are regarded as roughly the equivalent of an 'A' level. (These exams are NOT a substitute for GCSEs and 'A' levels if you are applying to a university but, like the LAMDA and Guildhall qualifications, they would be very good to have and to add to an application form.) It should be possible to take the Trinity College exams in some parts of the USA.

It is not necessary to take any of these exams to become a child actor. Many child actors have never taken such examinations in their lives. An examiner may well be looking for different abilities from those needed in a tv series or even in a tv commercial. On the other hand, grade exams do show a certain level of commitment and achievement, and the taking of them is likely to help boost confidence in self-presentation, public speaking and the like. In fact, this point is so significant that some ordinary schools are able to offer such exams as part of their teaching.

According to LAMDA, 'The purpose of the examination structure is not to burden students already weighed down by the demands of national examination programmes nor to encourage a sense of competition with peers. It is a way in which individuals can monitor their progress – often from an early age – in an area they enjoy and in which they feel motivated to move forward.

'In addition to providing a record of personal achievement, it can be a useful indication to prospective employers that an interest and determination to develop a high level of communication skills has been pursued and achieved.'

These are, I believe the most widely available exam systems for children in drama. There are other courses that may suit a particular child better. Nigel Rideout mentions another organisation in his book *First Steps towards an Acting Career*, The English Speaking Board, although 'not strictly theatre orientated [it] provides an invaluable service in improving standards of oral communication in most walks of life for students in further and higher education.' Again, there are some 'ordinary' schools where these exams are part of the curriculum.

The London College of Music and the Central School of Speech and Drama may also offer courses appropriate to the needs of different students.

There are several organisations that offer dance examinations. Again, these offer measures of progress and achievement. If I say little about them, it is because I have rarely needed dancers for television drama. Where there are dance sequences, we would usually employ a choreographer. In my experience, when dealing with young actors, choreographers look at what the individual can do at the audition rather than ask about grades. This is not to deny the use of grades but it suggests that examining boards are not necessarily measuring what we may be looking for.

For young actors of 16 or over, there are also B-tech courses in performing arts, equivalent to GCSE and 'A' level, and beyond, available at some sixth-form colleges and the like. The range of these and other courses is wide. Most are for over 16s and fall outside the scope of this book. For serious enquiries, Careers Advisers, Education Authorities, Public Libraries, the National Council for Drama Training, and Equity are all possible sources of information.

5 Rules, Regs and Licences

We cannot move when working with children without knowing about or referring to the rules and regulations. Whether or not a child gets a job depends on what the rules allow. Almost every situation you can think of that might arise when a child is acting has a law, rule or regulation attached to it.

Many local educational authorities generally have an Educational Welfare Officer. These are usually the people who deal with applications for licences – and they can turn applications down. They are also entitled to inspect a place where a child is working, whether performing, rehearsing or doing school work away from school. If they find something wrong or records not properly kept, they can have a child withdrawn from a production – even if this means cancelling the production. Understanding the rules is therefore important.

The second part of the chapter looks at comments about the rules from some of those who have experienced them in practice.

General rules for children working

The rules for children working in any job not involving performance make it clear that:

- children may not work under the age of 13;
- they may work for up to 2 hours on schooldays;
- they may work for up to 2 hours on Sundays;
- they may work for a maximum of 5 hours (if they are under 15) or 8 hours (if they are 15 or over) on Saturdays and weekdays during the school holidays, subject to an overall weekly limit of 25 hours or 35 hours, respectively, in the school holidays;
- they may not work more than 1 hour before the start of school;
- they may not work in school hours;
- they may not work before 7.00 in the morning or after 7.00 at night;

- they may not work for more than 4 hours without at least 1 hour's break;
- they must have an employment card from the local authority;
- they may not work in any industrial undertaking like a building site or a factory;
- they must not work at any job unless it is on the local authority list of jobs that 13-year-olds may do. This means that there will be some variation from one area to another. But anything that could harm health, well-being or education is banned;
- *Children must have a 2-week break from any work during the school holidays.*

The 'general' rules include two references to performing.

- *children may not take part in 'certain' theatrical performances without a licence issued by the local authority;*
- *children employed in sporting and advertising activities will be subject to licences as currently required for other performances.*

These rules are very restricting. The more specific rules on performing are restricting, too, but they do give a lot more room for children to work – especially for those under 13.

Rules for children working as performers

In the United Kingdom, there are over thirty pages of special rules governing any kind of professional performance. These rules are amended from time to time and you need to be aware how they affect you. The latest set of rules should mean that the law about child employment is more or less consistent across countries of the European Union.

The three rules in italic in the above list are recent and cause additional complications for Production Companies. Children's television has in the past frequently taken advantage of the summer holiday period for shooting as much material as possible. There are then more hours of daylight and no tuition is necessary, so we can be more flexible in the use of time, thus lessening the stress on both children and Production. Since tutors should not count any tuition period of less than 30 minutes towards the overall daily average total of 3 hours, and since SATS exams can take children away from the set for a couple of hours or more, it is obvious that holidays are preferable!

Another problem is that the rules used to allow children to work

4 days a year without a licence provided that they missed no school or were from a full-time stage school. This was extremely useful if we had crowd scenes: we could arrange for a stage school to send an assortment of children who had had little or no work in the previous months to our location. We did not have to book specific individuals up to 6 weeks ahead and produce masses of paperwork. It was good for us and gave the children concerned a little more experience. Now this concession has been removed the extra paperwork will be a problem certainly for smaller companies and those on an already tight budget.

Advertisers will also have problems. Many commercials are shot over one or two days. The 4-day rule gave the commercials companies great flexibility, allowing decisions to be made very close to their deadlines. Now, they will have to plan much further ahead.

Licences

Agents and the Production Companies should be familiar with both general and specific rules. However, a few general comments may be helpful.

- Most amateur performances do not need a licence.
- 'A child interviewed or filmed while taking part in some normal activity which has not been prearranged is probably not taking part in a performance within the meaning of the Act. On the other hand, if what a child does is directed in any way, this may convert the activity into a performance.' However, a school concert or a church service that happened to be filmed would probably also not need licensing.
- There is an absolute prohibition on dangerous performance. This means one in which 'life or limbs are endangered.'
- Any rehearsal on a performance day counts towards the hours worked on that day. A rehearsal on a day when there is no performance counts as a day for the purposes of the restrictions on the length of the working week. But it does not count as a performing day for the purposes of adding up the number of performing days used in a period of 12 months.

The following points are taken from The Law on Performances by Children – a guide to the Children (Performances) Regulations 1968 and related statutory provisions. These rules may change from time to time, and what follows is not definitive. What I have tried to do is to show what concerns the lawmakers and to give you a guide about some of the practical points that crop up most often.

Quotations are from the document. The rest is my paraphrasing or comment.

The licence for each child is issued by the local education authority covering the area where the child lives (or boards if at a boarding school). The licences are issued to '... the person responsible for the production in which the child is to take part.' This could include organisations such as the BBC or, for example, Carlton Television. The intent is that ' . . . the holder of the licence is the person who is responsible for observing the restrictions and conditions subject to which the licence is granted.'

There are two parts to each licence, one for the applicant, which is usually the Production Company, and the other for the parent.

The local authority may wish to contact the child's head teacher; to interview the child and the parent and to have the child medically examined. All this takes time, and the Production Company must allow at least 21 days before the date of the first performance or, preferably, before the first rehearsal. If this time is not allowed, the local authority has the power to turn down the application. Many authorities are short staffed in the area that deals with licence applications and need all the time they can get.

The application will show the overall dates a child will be needed, the place or places where rehearsals and performances will take place, the likely number of days or half days off school, the arrangements for tuition, the name of the chaperone and so on. **It is part of the whole idea of the regulations that it is actually necessary to have a child of a particular age playing the particular part, so some details of the part will also be included.**

If the child will be working in an area covered by a different local authority, then that authority will need a copy of information about the child.

The medical certificates, when they are needed, can be provided by the child's GP. There is usually a small charge for this. I do not recall any child I have wished to employ being turned down because of a medical problem. There was one girl I cast who had sickle-cell anaemia. Not only was she allowed to appear in my programmes, but she also went on to become a running character in *Grange Hill*. We were aware of the problem and allowed her to rest a little more than usual, when it was necessary.

The regulations say that local authorities must be satisfied that ' ... education shall not suffer' through a child being allowed to perform. It is the licence holder who is obliged to make suitable arrangements and to ensure that they are carried through. This usually means hiring a teacher who has been approved by a local authority. There is more about tutors later.

Everything is further complicated because the rules vary according to the child's age. As children get older, so the number of days and hours that they are allowed to work increases. Up to the 13th birthday the maximum allowance is 40 days per year. From 13 to school leaving age, sometime after the 16th birthday, the allowance goes up to a maximum 80 days a year. A local authority may refuse to allow a child to use up all possible days, and may take into consideration the number of rehearsal days required. There are circumstances in which these totals may be exceeded, but only with the express agreement of the local authority. Children of school age are required to average 3 hours a day of tuition in term-time. **This is usually the term of the local education authority where the child is actually working – not that of the child's own school.**

A child under 5 may work for a maximum of 30 minutes and may be at the place of performance or rehearsal for only 2 hours, those hours being between 9.30 a.m. and 4.30 p.m. This is why you frequently see the part of a baby being played by twins – we effectively double our working time that way. Any spare time must be used for meals, rest or recreation.

Children under 13 and over 5 are allowed up to 7½ hours in the workplace between 9.00 a.m. and 4.30 p.m. (or 5.00 p.m. if aged 10–12). They are allowed 3 hours of performance or rehearsal, working no more than 45 minutes at a time. If present for more than 3½ hours, they must have one break of at least 1 hour and another one of at least 15 minutes. On school days, they must also have 3 hours of education.

From 13 to the school leaving age, children are allowed an 8 hour day between the hours of 8.30 a.m. and 7.00 p.m. They may work for 1 hour without a break. If they are present for more than 4 hours, they must have one break of at least 1 hour and another of at least 15 minutes. Again, if it is a school day, they must have 3 hours' tuition.

Confusingly, there are exceptions to these rules for children of 12 and over. They can appear in tv studio productions that finish as late as 10 p.m.; they can work longer days, but fewer of them in a week.

It is also possible to arrange for children to work on location at night, if it is really necessary. In the summer, for instance, when it may stay light until nearly 10 p.m. an authority may allow night shooting beyond midnight. The child must then have a break of at least 16 hours before he can start work again; if he does night work on two consecutive nights he may not do any more night work for at least another week.' This is why a lot of night work with children takes place on Fridays; they have the weekend to recover.

A child may not work for more than 5 days in any 7 – but tuition can be done only on weekdays. This can make weekend working uneconomic.

The local authorities have no say in the financial arrangements made between a Production Company and a child, but they do have discretionary powers to 'safeguard the child's earnings'. They would, therefore, be sent a copy of the contract.

All those under school-leaving age must have someone 'in charge' of them. This can be a parent or grandparent or some other person approved by the licensing authority. Thus a parent or grandparent looking after his or her own child does not need a licence, but a sister (aged over 18) or ANY other person would.

It must be clear at all times who is responsible for a child. A child must be in the charge of a matron (or chaperone) 'throughout the engagement except at any time when he is in the charge of a teacher. A private teacher may act as a matron if he (or she) is approved as such by the licensing authority, provided that the number of children in his care when he is acting as matron does not exceed three.' The exception to this is where the child is travelling to or from home. The licence holder still has responsibility for what happens and is expected to organise suitable transport if necessary.

The regulations recognise that a matron, who may be appropriate for one child or group of children, may not be suitable for a different age group, or mix of sexes. The difference between working within a fixed routine like a theatre or tv studio production on the one hand and a film location on the other could mean that a matron might be accepted by the licensing authority for one type of job but not another.

'No child should be allowed to perform when unwell. If a child falls ill or is injured while in the charge of a matron or teacher, a doctor should be called and the licence holder must immediately notify the parent named on the application form and the local authority.'

Older children who are required to perform on 60 days or more must not be worked more than 8 weeks (40 days) before being given at least 14 days off.

No child is allowed to do any other work paid work on the day of performance or the day after.

The licence holder must keep a record for each child of the hours and days worked on a production and record the hours of tuition and breaks.

There are different rules for children working in the professional theatre.

Careful reading of the regulations shows that there is flexibility for the Production Company and an over-riding concern for the well-being of the child. It is easy to get carried away in the excitement of production, and for a director to lose track of the time, forgetting that the young actors may not have the stamina of adults. The rules are there to help the child actor and to keep them going for weeks at a time if necessary.

A NOTE TO ANYONE DEALING WITH A LICENCE FOR THE FIRST TIME

A well-run Production should have someone on the team who understands the licensing system. The responsibility for getting it right lies with the Production. All that the parent has to do is to answer questions truthfully and to deal with the forms without delay. If there are any problems, the agent should be able to help – the people at the agency will have experience of dealing with the paperwork and with local authorities.

Rules in other countries

Other countries have their own systems. Children are featured in all manner of films and tv productions. If a British child is employed on a production (British or otherwise) where the filming must be done abroad, the licence still has to be issued from this country, and British rules will apply unless the local rules are even more stringent – in which case they will apply. This parallels the system in the United States of America where each State is free to add to minimum federal laws if this will produce greater protection for the child.

There is a very helpful booklet produced jointly by the American Federation of Television and Radio Artists and the Screen Actors' Guild. It is called the AFTRA-SAG *Young Performers' Handbook* and would be invaluable for anyone working with a child likely to appear in America. I have included contact addresses for AFTRA and SAG at the end of this book.

Despite attempts to harmonise regulations throughout countries of the EU, there are still variations.

Is it all worth it? Is it even necessary?

'Yes,' is the short answer. Local authority inspectors do have the right to take children off the set of any licensed show, or any unlicensed show that should have had a licence. However, local education authorities are sending their inspectors to the sets less and less often. When I started directing children, we would see an inspector at least once or twice in a run. Now, it is common not to see any at all. Obviously, a long-running series with many children that is likely to be focused in one particular area is likely to receive visits. *Grange Hill*, for instance, has been recorded almost entirely in the vicinity of Borehamwood in Hertfordshire for over half of its life. The local inspector maintains a close working relationship with the Production.

Everyone I have talked to agrees that it is reasonable to protect children from exploitation. It is certainly very practical to have someone on the set just looking after the children. I think it is easy for the production team to become so wrapped up in what they are doing that they fail to notice that it is lunchtime, or time for a lesson, or time for a child to be sent home. Also, a stage, a film set, a location or a tv studio, all have heavy equipment, potentially dangerous machinery and lots of electrical gear lying around. It is a matter of common sense and safety to have someone protecting a child at all times.

Stephanie Manuel of Stagecoach said, 'I do believe children should be protected. On the other hand, perhaps the rules are a little too stringent. I know myself how strong and capable children are.'

Her experience of putting on non-professional stage shows is that children can work longer without a break than the rules suggest. I think she is right where there are perhaps only a few performances in a local theatre. The problems are more likely to show up if a child is expected to keep on working for weeks at a time. Regular breaks and relatively short days are necessary then. For example, I can remember one girl of 12 who was a brilliant natural actress and who used to get very tired at about 4.00 in the afternoon. It would have been unkind of me to ask her to go beyond 4.30 p.m. or to ask her to do anything really difficult so late in her day. Since that series, I have made a point of trying to schedule long or difficult scenes early in the day so we can get them out of the way while everyone is still fresh. This '12-year-old' is in her 30s now, still in the profession and still giving very subtle, natural performances.

Mr Vote, the vice-principal at the Italia Conti Academy made it clear that he thought the rules both necessary and effective.

Anna Scher is also firm about this. 'If a child gets a job, they've got to be properly licensed. The Law is there to protect the child against exploitation ... I just don't park on the yellow line – I never have. I don't want to; I don't want the children to.'

Production Companies are encouraged to put the lowest price they can on their productions, to undercut each other. There was a time when the BBC would allow 10 weeks to make a six-part serial. This is now down to about 7 weeks for a similar show. (In both cases we are talking about shooting with a single camera, largely on location.)

An independent company might reduce the price of its production by saying it would shoot in a six-week period. There are various tricks we use to reduce the amount of time a child is on the set, by using stand-ins for example – but they increase costs, of course. We can simplify the shooting as much as possible and also refuse to do retakes except for major disasters. In my view, both these measures, rigidly and uniformly enforced, will reduce the quality of the finished show. Even then, it is hard to see how a company can stick to all the restrictions on hours AND give proper tuition to any child who is heavily featured in such a series. It is an increasing problem and local education authorities have fewer resources to spare to inspect shoots in their areas.

In view of all this, I asked about the pressure on agencies from such companies. Characteristically, Anna Scher said, 'I just won't play ball with them. It's as simple as that ... Casting directors will try and push me. The more they push me, the more I'm strengthened in my resolve to do it the right way.'

At the Junior Television Workshop in Nottingham, Ian Smith felt the law on hours was reasonable and ' . . . the amount of days that kids work is about right. The only thing I would say is that the 80 days could disrupt a child's educational life in a secondary school. But, obviously, when it's balanced out by tutoring on set, I'd hope one could limit the damage. We'd be naïve to say there isn't going to be some area where there is going to be some disruption.'

The disruption can be counterbalanced by the positive experience of working with adults in a challenging and demanding way. This is often true of 'one-off' projects that happen partly in school holidays. I asked Ian Smith about the longer-running series, where a child may be involved for large parts of several years. 'I think there is the potential for serious educational disruption. I think I'd bring back OUR responsibility to ensure that the GCSE years are, as far as possible, untouched. The ones that tend to get the lead parts are, generally speaking, high achievers. Grades may be affected a little but, ultimately, it won't disrupt their chances of going to university.'

Like Anna Scher, Ian has taught in comprehensive schools. Unlike most agents, these two do take classes themselves, and therefore know most of their students very well. The attitude of care that I noted in my interviews with them perhaps stems from this.

Parents may work as chaperones but there are problems. It is easy for the parent to be ignorant of the rules. Such a parent is likely to allow the Production to do anything it may ask. Similarly parents may be pushing their children too hard. Quite a lot of child actors move into acting from modelling. A lot of child models begin as babies or toddlers. This can only be because it is the parents' decision to put their child to work. It is not unknown for such parents to be pushy and concerned very much with what the child can earn.

Mr Vote tells the story of a commercial where a chaperone was looking after the child, but the parents were present at the end of the scheduled day. The child was tired but the commercial was not completed. The chaperone (quite rightly) stopped the child working – '... therefore stopping the shoot. The parents were horrified. "What have you done?" asked one. "My child will never work again." This was not the case. The shoot had been under-scheduled.' The company recognised they had made a mistake and set up a second day's shoot. The rules are necessary and are there for the child's benefit. We all need to remember this.

In practice?

The regulations are occasionally phrased flexibly. If a Production gets into difficulty, because of bad weather, perhaps, the authorities can use some discretion, and so can chaperones. For instance, if it is impossible for a child to complete its part within the permitted 40 or 80 days – and if the child has not used any days on any other productions, it is possible for the authority to grant a limited increase but the whole emphasis is on the welfare of the child.

I think it is rare for children to suffer from working for any of the major companies who employ them. I think education in the precise terms of the National Curriculum may be set back a little, from time to time. On the other hand, I think many children learn a great deal about their own strengths and abilities to cope in responsible ways with adult demands. This amounts to another form of 'education'.

As for the rules ... On a film location, it is quite difficult sometimes to define when a child is or is not working – we rehearse for 10 minutes, then there is a pause whilst tape is reloaded. We shoot for 2 minutes then there is a pause whilst we reset. We shoot for another 2 minutes then we move the camera, which may take 2 minutes or 40, if there is a relight. So it goes on. Overall, I think it is fair to say that most productions stick to the spirit of the law, but regularly bend the rules without harm to children. As pressure increases on budgets and schedules, this rule bending is likely to become law breaking. It is already quite common to hear of productions where children have missed their full allocation of tuition and, as inspections decrease in frequency, hours will be stretched even more.

The experiences of some children suggests that things are far from ideal:

Tom Szekeres, who worked with me on *The Demon Headmaster*, thinks the system can work well. 'It all evens out,' he says, 'and as tuition is one-to-one, you get loads more done.'

Frances Amey found tuition boring on the shoot but '... when you get back to school, you're glad you haven't missed out on what everyone else was doing.'

On the matter of hours, most of the children agree that regulation is a good thing. There are examples of law breaking – even though no-one has told me they feel that they have suffered as a result! One boy, who is now over 16 said, 'I can't ever remember being taken off the set because they'd gone over hours. I think a lot of chaperones are quite liberal. I remember being on set till 2 o'clock in the morning, with 6 o'clock starts.'

I queried this. There are minimum breaks after night shooting, and no-one under 16 should ever be starting at 6.00 a.m. The response was clear. 'I started at 6 loads of times. I've been on set at 6.'

A more common experience was to be picked up at 7 or just after to be at location in time for breakfast. 'Not that we started before 9. It was just to get you there.'

Something that under 16s often ask is whether they are entitled to be paid overtime. This implies that numbers of children do truly do overtime. At the chaperone's discretion, a Production is occasionally allowed to work on an extra half-hour, particularly if this will reduce the load on the concerned children another day. Apart from that, children should not be doing overtime at all. Legally speaking, payment of overtime amounts to an admission of law breaking!

Children given leading parts in any form of play or film will be stretched. It is said that some stress can be good for you. Here, I think 'stress' has a meaning closer to 'challenge' than to 'tension and anxiety'. But there have been cases of children finding the whole experience too much for them.

About twenty years ago, there was a girl who had her own series and who later had a breakdown linked to an eating disorder. She was at one of the full-time stage schools. Such problems, apparently, are rare. Eating disorders can affect any pupil in any school at any time. This girl's head teacher had only come across three such cases in all his time at a stage school. I believe this is actually a lot better than the average for most other types of school. It seems unlikely that the problems this girl faced were due to shortcomings in the law. Nonetheless, the questions should be asked, 'Is this Production going to put too much strain on this child. Should we find a different child? Should we modify the nature of the child's part? Should we modify the schedule?'

At the end of the day – it's only entertainment. It is not worth screwing up your life for it!

6 *Tutors, Chaperones, Matrons and Mothers ...*

... come in all shapes and sizes. When there are only a couple of children in a project, and when they are mostly on the set (or off it) together, there is no reason why the tutor should not also be the chaperone. It is normal for a tutor-chaperone to be paid more than a tutor, and for a tutor to be paid more than a chaperone. In my experience, a chaperone is paid more than a parent looking after her or his own child.

A chaperone needs no specific qualifications. A tutor has to be a fully trained teacher. In this country, in order to register as a tutor the candidate has to quote the DfEE number (this used to be known as the DES number), which is given on qualification by the Department for Education and Employment.

Chaperones and others

Sometimes, you will see the word 'matron' used instead of the word 'chaperone', especially in the older official documents. There is no difference and I have used the word 'chaperone' throughout this book (except occasionally in the previous chapter). In terms of the rights and responsibilities in keeping a production to its obligations, a chaperone and, say, a mother are equal. I suspect, however, that an experienced chaperone is going to feel more confident in telling a production that a child needs a rest 'now' than a mother who has never been on the set before. I suspect, too, that it is easier for children in the charge of professional chaperones to mix together on equal terms than it is where some have a parent present and some do not.

Each child is the responsibility of a named chaperone. No child should be left at a place of work without that chaperone.

Twenty years ago, I met on elderly lady who was very sweet, but she literally could not keep up with her charges. Another chaperone on a colleague's production was very young. She clearly lacked authority enough to stop her charges chasing her down the hotel corridor with a soda siphon. I have also seen one chaperone screaming into the face of an 11-year-old 'extra' because he had the temerity to take an extra piece of fruit from the catering table at the end of lunch without her express permission. She didn't work with me again.

These days, I think there is generally a more professional approach. Certainly on *Grange Hill*, last time I was anywhere near it, the chaperones were all very experienced and knew exactly what they were doing. They worked well together and were easily able to cope with their charges. If there are any concerns on series like this, it is for those who have crossed the 16-year-old threshold. It is with those who have just attained a new freedom that problems of self-discipline may arise.

Although all chaperones and tutors have to have a licence from their local authority, the vetting that each authority applies will vary. We tend to take people we know again and again or to interview new people on recommendation from colleagues. I would expect my Production Manager or First Assistant to choose the chaperones, and not simply to take those pushed towards us by a stage school or agent. I would be wary about booking a chaperone from one agency to look after children from different agencies because of concerns over favouritism.

In general, I would hope that the chaperone and the children would be from similar backgrounds. Most chaperones are women. It can be helpful to have a male chaperone when there are adolescent boys in the cast.

In this country, it would be normal to have a chaperone looking after one or more children. In the USA, I believe it is the right of parents to look after their own children. I discourage this, because I think that children from about 8 years upwards will work more freely without 'mother breathing down their necks'. Also, if you have a dozen children it is cheaper and more sensible to have two full-time chaperones treating all equally than half a dozen mothers, all trying to make their own mark. I would go for two chaperones if there were more than about three children. On a long shoot, it is unlikely that all the children need to be on the set at once, and one chaperone cannot be in two places at once.

The selection of the chaperone becomes particularly important when the children need to stay away from home. Then the chaperone really will be *in loco parentis*. The chaperone will be the one getting up in the middle of the night if somebody cannot sleep. I think it fair to give the parents as much contact as possible with the chaperone in cases like this – even if it is only over the phone. It helps everyone if the parents have confidence in the carer!

If there is any ferrying around to be done, we make sure that the chaperone can drive. If necessary, we will provide a people-carrier for her to drive. When this has happened on my productions, we have also given space off the road, when necessary, for the chaperone to familiarise herself with driving such a vehicle.

The system works well, but I do think parents must be free to ask about anything they are concerned about.

Tutors

Tutors must be qualified teachers. I would try and ensure that the tutor had experience of teaching the age group of children in my cast, which can mean we look for teachers with experience at both primary and secondary level. Some teachers start tutoring because it fits in with their life style to be able to take short engagements when it suits them. Some have taken early retirement and find the change of pace on a film or television location is stimulating. The schedule often requires long periods away from home and this may not suit everyone.

If the ages of the children were mixed, a tutor would not be teaching more than half a dozen children. As I have already said, we would expect our tutors to talk to each child's school to sort out the work to be covered in each subject during the run of the project. This means that each tutor has to be prepared to teach – or at least to supervise – all subjects. This does not mean they need to be experts in all subjects. The teaching of practical science is, of course, difficult on location – but not always impossible for a science teacher. If a school cannot or will not provide the information, then it is up to the tutor to devise a curriculum.

Tutoring of this kind can be very positive. A child can get a lot of attention. Teaching may even be one-to-one. It becomes easy to say, 'I've never understood decimals.' Long-standing puzzles may at last be sorted out. There is often good progress and real motivation.

The problems really arise with the pressure on budgets. If I have to reduce my budget, I may be forced to shorten my schedule. This means I must shoot more material each day. In its turn, this means that children heavily involved in the project are less likely each day to achieve their target of three hours' tuition. They may find there is insufficient time to complete their set work.

Tuition on set.

Concerns

I have worked with one of the few tutors with science qualifications, Lina Wright. She has observed these cutbacks with alarm, and she sent me some thoughts on the subject, from which I quote.

'Over the past few years, I have become increasingly aware that there is not enough time being allowed in filming schedules to give children three hours' tuition per day. This is apparent as soon as I am given the schedule ... when it's quite obvious that on most days the principal child is used in all the scenes.

'The schedule seems to be planned without taking into account either the educational needs of the child, or the fact that three hours' tuition per day is actually required by law. Of course, it is obvious that any schedule is subject to change due to unforeseen circumstances ... so to expect the child to have three hours' tuition each and every day is unrealistic. However, there have been several occasions when a whole week goes by and filming goes exactly according to the schedule and the child is filming most of the time with very few breaks for tuition.

'This sometimes happens in a long shoot and everything is fine if there is then an opportunity to catch up with tuition during another week when the child is not working so much. This is quite acceptable since the total number of hours of tuition over the whole shoot is what really counts. However, when there is no time allowed for catching up, overall tuition hours are hopelessly inadequate.

'I have raised the above points on several productions and I have always got the same answer: more money is needed to allow for a longer filming schedule.

'Why do children taking part in a production need tuition anyway?

'Quite simply, because if one stops doing a particular activity, one loses the skill. It is also important to maintain the discipline of having to concentrate on work set by teachers from the child's own school for the following reasons:

- it maintains the child's contact with their school;
- it reassures the child that he/she will be keeping up with their friends in school subjects;
- it shows the child's teachers (and parents) that the Production Company values the child's education and is ensuring that the child does not think that filming is the only priority in life.

'Although it can be argued that the filming environment is itself an enriching experience and some programmes, especially those set in a particular historical period or location, are actually of educational value in themselves, this does not help the child to pass a maths or science exam when he returns to school. Insufficient tuition while filming may lead to failure at school and subsequent loss of confidence and alienation from peers. Between the ages of 14 and of 16, adequate tuition is essential otherwise lower GCSE grades may affect a child throughout adult life.'

Lina would like to recommend attention to several factors:

1 the recognition of the importance of the child's educational needs, recognition of the fact that filming is a small part of a child's life and recognition that education is a continuous process which is damaged when interrupted.

2   the involvement of the tutor at the planning stage so that tuition
    can be worked into the schedule to make best use of ALL the time
    available.
3   the provision of a tutorial room or other suitable space close to
    the set so that even small gaps in shooting can be used for tuition.
4   co-operation from the crew and production team as the tutor
    tries to keep the child interested in his schoolwork while being
    surrounded by the exciting world of the film set. This can be
    difficult. Tuition time is vital to keep the child's 'feet on the
    ground'. It is a time when the child moves from the artificial
    world of show business back to the familiar world of education.

She concludes: 'Provided that the child's education does not suffer,
working on a film production can be an enormously enriching experience for children. They learn to relate to adults and begin to understand the responsibility needed to work in an adult environment.
They learn self-discipline and consideration for other people. In quite
a few productions I have worked on, the children have become more
mature and have also done very well in exams on their return to
school because they have benefited from one-to-one tuition. This
ideal outcome should be kept in mind in the planning stages of a
production.'

Children are under increasing pressure – even in former bastions
of correctness like the BBC where schedules can be so short that
getting continuous periods of thirty minutes becomes difficult.

Each child is different. Some achieve great academic AND acting
success, but to do this, the child's career needs to be managed carefully. It may be a case of not taking on – or not trying to get – too
many engagements!

Lina's ideal outcome may be difficult to achieve. With more
channels – more television chasing a finite amount of advertising
revenue, with even the BBC spreading its resources ever more thinly,
the problems are likely to increase – or maybe children will be take a
lesser part in children's drama. That would be a pity.

Pushy parents

I have found myself quoting several people on the importance of education. Lina came across one mother who did not see the importance
of tuition for her boy. Lina told her that there was no choice. 'The
boy was going to have to do the three hours and that was that …
I think it was the first job where the child had had tutoring. It just

came as an enormous shock that he HAD to do it … There was the discipline that you come off the set and you go straight to tuition and you work very hard.'

This led me to ask about the nightmare 'stage mother'. 'Some of them,' Lina replied, 'are incredibly pushy. The child is where he is only because the mother has pushed.'

She also told me a story about one of her first productions, which confirms my doubts about having parents as chaperones. There were two boys in an adult drama. Lina was tutor-chaperone for both. But one of the fathers would come and chaperone as well. The younger boy, aged 11, had the major part. 'The production wanted to keep them incredibly long hours. And, of course, when they'd got the father there, the production asked his permission. I was only there *in loco parentis*. So there was nothing I could do about it except say, "Well, he's not really supposed to …" Some companies prefer to have the parents there, especially parents who don't know the rules.

'What made this situation worse was the attitude of the mother. The boy had been pushed into the filming because, as his mother said – in front of him, "You've got to do well in this because you've got to get another part because we need more money." '

Fortunately, not all parents behave in this way. Lina redressed the balance:

'Some mothers make excellent chaperones for their own children. They are well informed about the rules and besides ensuring that their children are well looked-after, they also make sure that the child is well behaved and responsible during filming.

'I have also come across several parents who by careful management of their children's career actually ensure that, besides acting, the child gets a very good education and goes on to do a university degree. Of the children I have tutored with established acting careers, two have gone to Oxford and one to Cambridge.'

If there is a problem, it is good to talk about it. Lina had one girl who was worried because she was falling behind with the work her school had set (the production was not allowing sufficient tuition time). Lina was able to talk to the school and assure them that the girl was working really hard and doing her best – but there were a lot of subjects for her to cover. The school was very understanding and the girl even won a prize at the end of her year for effort. When it comes to problems, if the communication is good, 'We can sort it out.'

Lina works mainly as a tutor, but she is also a licensed chaperone. She says, 'I think to attempt to do 3 hours a day is very sensible. I had to renew my chaperone's licence a little while ago, so I had to go to my local authority. When it came to tuition, [the Education Officer] said, "It's not the end of the world if you don't make the 3 hours as long as you're always trying to achieve that." What was more important than anything was the child's overall welfare. And I've already taken this attitude myself.'

We moved on to talk about the 40 and 80 day rules. I asked Lina if she thought these limits were about right. 'Definitely. Forty days is sensible for under 12s because it is important for them to be in an environment with people their own age. Over 12s are better able to cope with the adult world, but too long an absence from school would affect their education.'

Both Lina and I have worked on productions where a child chosen for a part could not take it up because he or she did not have enough licensed days left, in spite of what the agent had said. She said, 'If some children were very good, they'd just be used all the time. And if children act all the time when they're young, they close the door to everything else that could come with their education.'

I told Lina about the people – especially in stage schools – who had said that if they were not acting as children, they might never get the chance again. 'No,' said Lina. 'No, there are lots of drama clubs. They don't HAVE to go to stage school.'

I asked Lina about 16 being the cut-off point for compulsory tuition on the set. 'I think that it's perfectly all right, if they've decided they want to carry on acting, they don't really need tuition any more … They've got to make a choice. They know that they can't do 'A' levels and get strings of As AND spend most of their time acting.'

We talked about the difficulties of mixing teenagers of 15½ and those over 16. 'One minute you're all over them and "getting them to bed by nine o'clock" and the next day, it's "do what you want when you want!"'

'It's very difficult when you've got 'children' under age and 'children' over age. This is especially true when the 16-year-olds '… are wanting to drink and go out and all the rest of it … But that's where, in your job as chaperone and tutor, you earn your money.'

Responsibility

Staying away on location, a chaperone is responsible for a child or for several children, twenty-four hours a day. The children are there to do a job on a project that may be costing a million or more pounds, and it is the production that is paying for the chaperone. There are horror stories of chaperones leaving their children and going off for a drink, even of a child found wandering 'in the middle of the road and the chaperone nowhere to be found'. It is a great responsibility.

All kinds of things MAY happen on a film set. All kinds of people work in the business; there may be swearing (but no worse than in the playground); there may be people of all sexual persuasions; there may be drugs. But we employ chaperones to protect children from all this.

If you are going to let your child take part in a film or tv production – and, if your child really wants to and has the chance, then it is probably the right thing to allow it. But, as Lina says, 'Find out everything you can about what care is going to be taken of your child. I think that it's very important that you do talk to the child, to the chaperone, to the production. And if the chaperone is any good, if a parent is concerned, the chaperone should be able to put parents' minds at rest. But if the chaperone isn't any good or if she doesn't know her job, then the parents should complain.'

7 *Getting a Job*

So, you go to classes, you have an agent, you even have a photograph in *Children's Spotlight*. How do you get a job?

You don't, really. That is, YOU do not get yourself a job, you do not simply apply for a part and get it. It is all far more complicated than that and, for anyone under 16, the whole process will take weeks.

There are young people (and parents) who write to directors asking for work. The problem is that most of the letters will arrive at a point when the director is also looking for work, or is just finishing his or her last job, or has not even begun thinking about auditions. If she or he is thinking about auditions, the letter writer is likely to be the wrong age, living in the wrong part of the country or perhaps with no useful experience, just enthusiasm. By the wrong part of the country, I mean simply that a director may be seeking someone with either a particular regional accent or what is called RP (Received Pronunciation – some people used to call this BBC English.) If you have the wrong accent for a particular project, you stand no chance of getting the part. It is rare that children can sustain an accurate accent that is not their own. On the other hand, most adult actors are able to act convincingly in at least two or three 'voices'. If you speak with 'Received Pronunciation' but live far from the area where the project will be made, you are unlikely to be chosen because the cost of providing hotels and suitable travel arrangements. There are usually enough RP speakers in any given area to give directors plenty of choice, most of the time.

Of course, if you happen to hear that a director wants an unusual combination of skills such as being able to ride a horse, play the flute and act, and you happen to combine these skills, then you may find a letter or call to the Production Company is worthwhile. Such occasions are rare.

When you are hoping for a part, it is worth remembering that the director is going to see dozens of other under-16s for that part. Therefore, dozens minus one will be disappointed. There is a contrast here between getting even a small speaking part and being a support-ing artist or extra.

Look at it from the director's point of view: whatever the project, the starting point will usually be a script. The script will usually define the characters required in terms of age, sex, personality and accent.

From the script, the director will prepare a 'cast breakdown'. This is simply a list of all the characters needed with the details specified in the script. It should also have production dates and show the involve-ment of each child – the likely number of performance days needed, and where the child will be expected to perform. This tells the agent if there are likely to be problems with a child being away from home for any length of time. If there are several children, there may be a separate list of children's parts. A copy of this list will be sent to agents and stage schools in the area where the production is to be based.

The schools and agents will then send in details, usually with photographs, of all the children matching the breakdown, who are available for the dates shown and who have enough performance days.

I do not know how many agents and stage schools, full- and part-time, there are in the UK. They do seem to have a bush telegraph. If we send out a dozen breakdowns to reliable agents, then you can be sure that the phone and fax lines will soon be humming with other agents wanting breakdowns, too.

The difficulty is that most agents have individuals on their books who may well be right for something – who may even be exception-ally good in the right part. There is not enough time to see every child suggested by every agent. I do try agents new to me, but I do tend to try first those where I have been successful before, spreading the net wider only as it is necessary.

I was hoping to find a boy with a light northern accent for one production. I gave the details to all the usual agents, and also travelled to Leeds and Nottingham to see a number of boys in each city. I was also seeing girls because I needed a pair of fraternal twins, that is a boy and a girl. In the end, the 'single' boy I chose spoke with Received Pronunciation and had a London base. The twins presented a prob-lem. None of the boys matched any of the girls but one agent had a pair of real twins. In the end, I chose them and they did a good job for me. However, one of the Nottingham girls read another part very well. She had a Nottingham accent, which I did not want for a girl living in 'Wessex', but she was so good that I decided the accent I grew up with would be fine.

The really unfortunate thing about these auditions was that although I saw about fifty children the boy I finally chose was the second I saw on the first day of casting and the twins were about the fourth appointment on the same day. It happens like that sometimes. Another boy I saw at the first casting had travelled up from the West Country. I eventually turned him down but he later played major parts, first in the ITV film version of *The Story of the Treasure Seekers*, loosely based on the book by E. Nesbit, and then in the BBC adaptation of *The Phoenix and the Carpet,* also by E. Nesbit. The fact that he came from so far away did not stop his getting work, but it did mean long journeys for some fruitless auditions!

If I need only three or four characters, I will ask the agents to send their clients to me in West London. The agent who sends in only three names is just as likely to get someone through as the one who sends in fifty. Usually, I will go to some of the full-time stage schools and see several of their clients on their home ground. In fact, I am very likely to do the rounds of the London stage schools every time I am setting up a new project, because there is usually a requirement for several children.

Even though I may initially reject a child I am quite happy to see the same child in succeeding years. People develop; their abilities can grow. A 9-year-old may be just a little too young and not quite right this year. Next year, he may be fine. I am also prepared to work on successive productions with the same children (and staff – and actors!) if they are 'right'. I remember one girl at Jackie Palmer's in High Wycombe whom I picked out in three successive years for very different stories. I did not choose her because I had worked with her before – she just fitted each part better than the 'opposition'.

If the story is regionally based, or if there is a character who could have a regional accent, I contact any stage school or agent I am aware of in the area. Manchester, Birmingham and Leeds are only three examples of cities with specialist agencies. Nottingham and Birmingham also have Children's Television Workshops.

In areas under-represented by agents, I will try local schools with a good reputation for drama. In this way, children with no previous experience of television and no long-term interest in becoming actors may find themselves on national television.

You will see from all this that chance plays a big part in getting even a first audition.

Auditions

What can you expect at a first audition? They do vary a lot. Frances Amey remembers, 'When I went to my first audition ever, I was really excited and spent hours wondering what to wear. I turned up quite dressed up and was surprised to find no-one else had bothered!'

Broadly speaking, there are two kinds of audition, one is 'group', and the other is 'individual'. What you may expect will depend more on the individual director or casting director than on the kind of part you are going for. We all have our methods, which we change to fit particular circumstances. I sometimes work with small groups and sometimes with individuals.

Individual auditions

I may see an individual child for a part for a number of reasons. It may be that particular child is the only one represented by a particular agent whose other clients are all adults. The child may have commitments that prevent his or her attending a group audition. The child may have been ill or on holiday – or even working on another production when I saw the other children from the same agent. Occasionally the child may not be part of any organisation but has parents who have convinced me that it is worthwhile for us to meet. It may simply be that the child lives in an awkward place and can only conveniently manage one particular day and time.

Usually, I will try and cover the same ground that I do in a group audition. I will ask each child for age and birthday and about any productions previously undertaken. I'll then explain something about the project, and the part in the scene we are about to read. Before we get round to the reading, we may do an improvisation together. It is probable that one of my team will be with me, to whom I may hand over my part in the improvisation. Then we will read a scene from the script. I usually ask for some alternative reading of a line or, with a short scene, I may ask for a reading of the scene stressing a different emotion. This is not because the first reading is 'wrong' but because it tells me a lot about the child's flexibility and communication skills.

We make notes as we do in the group auditions, and then add the most suitable candidates to the shortlist. I don't think there is any particular advantage or disadvantage for the children involved in attending either this type of interview or the group audition.

Group auditions

'Group', here, can mean anything from 'more than two' to 'several hundred'. Sometimes, a Production will hold what is called an Open Audition. Children of the right age and ability will be invited to a specific place (with a suitable adult) and with no pre-selection by the Production. Children may even turn up in response to an advertisement in *The Stage*. There were open auditions like this for the film version of *Annie*. Each child then has the attention of the person responsible for casting for a few seconds and a quick decision is made, usually negative. Sometimes, a Production may see thousands of young hopefuls for a small number of parts.

A lot of talent will slip through the net this way, but the production will get lots of publicity.

A smaller version of this kind of audition might be for a television commercial. Children, usually from agencies, will be sent in quite large numbers to a particular venue. The initial sorting will then be just on appearance. It is no good going along in your best suit or dress if an urchin is needed, or in your torn jeans if a Little Lord Fauntleroy is needed. Normally, the advertising agency will send a brief to the stage schools and agencies, but things may change at the last minute. All you can do is to think positive and be yourself!

Daniel told me that advertising auditions were exciting, but not always fun. 'You wait two hours, then they look at your face and say, "You can go now." It's the same with modelling.'

Mass auditions have been described as boring and likely to be poorly organised and unsatisfactory. The one advantage is that you are not kept waiting to be told you will not be needed. Rachael Goodyer makes the point here, though, that bad news may be better taken if it is given by someone you know, such as your agent.

Gunnar Cauthery was called to an audition for a commercial. 'I travelled up to London in the rush hour for an audition where I read no script – they simply wanted to see what I looked like. I was angered by this because the return ticket cost me £25.00, which I couldn't really afford, and I wasted half a day which could have been spent meeting any one of several urgent deadlines.'

Charlotte had had another bad experience. 'Five of us went in and they said, "Smile." And that was it! It was just on looks – that's the worst type of audition.'

Nicola added, 'It's really frustrating when they do that for acting parts. Someone gets the part and you watch them and think, "I could have done that better." Or "I could have cut my hair if they'd asked me."'

I have heard several people refer to auditions like these as 'cattle markets.'

Anna Scher will not allow her children even to audition for commercials.

I usually plan to see about fifty children for each major part I cast. If there are eight children, then I am likely to see 400 – or more. It is not possible to sit in my office and make 400 appointments of even ten minutes each. It is getting more and more difficult for children to take time off school to come to auditions, and my time, too, is limited. The way round this is for me to hold group auditions. These may be in three main types of location:

FULL-TIME STAGE SCHOOL OR PART-TIME SCHOOL

My first stop will usually be at some of the full-time stage schools and larger part-time schools. These organisations will have selected the students who they think best match my requirements.

Usually, I will be given groups of six to eight children of both sexes and mixed ages. Occasionally, I might be given a really large group of thirty or forty to see. I was once given one hundred children to see in two hours. That was ridiculous. The agent knew I had only a limited time, and I could not possibly do each child justice. This is the one and only time that any of my auditions may have felt like a cattle market. I have taken care not to be caught like that again.

Sometimes, at the part-time schools, I may be asked to watch a class going through a drama exercise, usually involving improvisation. In this case, I usually select a number of students who seem to have some potential and then take them through one my auditions. This is how things work at the Anna Scher Theatre.

Auditions at the full-time stage schools tend to happen in school time while, at the part-time schools, it will usually be after 4 p.m.

SCHOOLS

I often arrange to go to an ordinary school. This is usually because I am looking for a child with a particular accent. If I am doing a period piece, I may need a child with Received Pronunciation, in which case I may try private schools.

Usually, the school I visit will have a particularly strong drama department. The head of drama will select a group of children for me to see and auditions will generally take place within the school day – sometimes over the lunch break.

CENTRAL

Some of the agencies have clients scattered over a wide area. They often prefer to send children to me. In this case, I will often ask groups of six or eight to turn up together. Although they may not know each other, they will know that they are all from the same agency. I will also usually be able to arrange that each group has boys and girls as well as a spread of ages. The content of the auditions will be similar to that for the school groups.

Auditions – a director's point of view

ROUND 1

Time is limited, but it is important to try and get to know something about each child as quickly as possible. Whenever possible, I work with a colleague who may spot something I miss – or remember something I have forgotten. One or both of us will make notes from this stage onwards.

I begin by asking children individually for name, age and birthday. I will then ask what kind of work they have done or what shows at school. Sometimes, the answers can be surprising. I was working my way through a group and turned to one boy. 'And have you done any professional work?' I asked.

'Oh yes,' he replied.

'What?' I said.

Cheerfully, he asked, 'Have you got all afternoon?'

His list of films and tv series and plays was extensive and impressive, but did not take much longer to describe than those of his colleagues. Oddly enough, he did get the part!

I remember seeing another lad, some years ago. He, too, had an impressive c.v. The only thing was that all of his credits had been before he was 9. When I saw him, he was about 12. When I asked about the gap, he said, 'Yes, I've been out of the business for a while.'

This is a remark we normally hear only from adult actors. I should have resisted my impulse to say, 'Oh, I see. Are you making a comeback then?'

He was not thrown at all.

'Yes,' he said.

The list of credits does not make much difference to me unless it includes a performance I have seen. I have often given major parts to children with no previous television or professional experience. And I have long doubted the relevance to acting ability of a list of commercials that may range from Smarties to Birdseye. In any case, children grow up and change very quickly. Quirks and mannerisms that may be sweet or charming in an 8-year-old can look grotesque in a 13-year-old just starting to shave!

The purpose of the questions is really to hear what the children sound like and to begin to gauge their personalities. If any child seems to have nothing to say, I'll carry on asking questions.

Improvisation

When I am satisfied I'll ask the group to split into pairs or trios and to prepare a short improvisation. This means that I offer a situation to each small group and ask them to act out a little story about that situation. Each child must have a character and a purpose in the story, and will have to make up the words to tell the character's particular part of the story as the improvisation moves along. One simple situation I might offer is this, 'Suppose two of you are standing at a bus stop. The third comes along and asks the way to somewhere specific – perhaps somewhere local that really you all know. One of you is simply trying to be helpful and gives directions that are actually wrong. The other interrupts and tries to give correct directions.'

Such situations give me a chance to look at invention, believability and concentration. Sometimes, I walk around the improvising group as they are acting. It bothers me if actors start watching me rather than each other. Experience suggests they would be easily distracted on set, where there are many more distractions. I remember one boy tossing an imaginary coin. That was not special. The other boy followed the 'coin' with his eyes up into the air and back down again so convincingly that I employed him on my next two drama projects.

Obviously, in an improvisation much depends on your partners – not only how good they are, but how generous they are in giving you space to act. If a child has clearly been disadvantaged in a group improvisation like this, I can generally find time to have another go, often improvising myself directly with the child. This is probably unusual – there is not often time for this kind of second chance in most auditions.

Reading

The next step is a reading. I will hand out a scene from the script I am about to direct and ask the group to read from it. If I have a scene for three children, then I will have been working up to this point with six children; if the scene has four children, then I will have been working with groups of eight. There will be enough copies of the script for each child to have his or her own copy, and for me to hear the scene read twice with different children. The scenes are usually quite short, and there is enough time for all the children to read the scene through quietly before I ask for the 'out loud' reading. I also explain what the scene is about and what the characters might be feeling.

This tells me a lot about how natural each child sounds whilst saying someone else's words. Usually, I will then ask each of the children to read one or other of their lines again, but to try and put across a meaning different from the one they have already given me – even if that reading was suitable. This tells me something about how quickly a child can respond to my notes and gives me an idea about the child's abilities to give different 'readings' to a line.

As I go, I make notes about the quality of the improvisations, concentration, the appearance and sound of each child. The names of any children whose abilities stand out, I asterisk. If they stand out and seem right for one part in particular, I may give them a second scene to read, concentrating on that part. Usually, I try and keep an open mind at this stage.

In 1981, I was directing a serialisation of E. Nesbit's book, *The Story of the Treasure Seekers*. As auditions drew to a close, there were individuals who stood out in my mind. I had a rough plan for casting the six brothers and sisters, depending on which boy was strongest as the eldest brother, Oswald. Both my front runners were over 13, and had a lot going for them. When we held the second auditions, the producer Paul Stone and I had different thoughts. Whilst he liked the performances of the older boys, he much preferred a 12-year-old in the part. This was a lad I had been planning to cast as Dickie, the second brother. Because the tone of the book demands a certain amount of innocence, I finally agreed that the 12-year-old Simon Hill was the best Oswald. This meant all my other ideas needed revision. In effect, the best of the rest all got moved up a place in the family! Since then, I have been wary about making up my mind too early.

Once all the children have read, we move on to the next group. Personally, I always try and give everyone the same chance. I don't stop the 'hopeless' case and simply move on. I know that an audition is a big thing for some people. It is wrong to be dismissive. You never know which terribly nervous bud may turn into next year's blossom!

We quite often take Polaroid pictures of the children we are auditioning, sometimes singly, sometimes in a group. I try to 'snap' them against a simple scale so we can identify relative heights. These photographs are obviously more up to date than any others and help us remember more clearly the children we meet.

At the end of the session, we compare notes and mark our lists with comments, adding asterisks against the most promising. We then draw up a shortlist, grouping all those who scored one or more asterisks against the part for which they are most suitable.

What I look for at auditions is the individual who makes the part come alive from the page. Good reading ability is only a part of this. If I sense a problem with reading, I put more weight on the improvisations. I will also try and give a reading myself of a particular line and see how close the child can get to that. Also, if the first reading has been difficult, I will ask to hear part of the scene again, after going over difficult words or phrases myself. Frankly, if the child can neither pick up the dialogue 'by ear' quickly nor read fluently, there is likely to be a major problem when we come to shooting.

I suppose what we directors all want is a 'natural' actor − natural as in 'with in-built ability' as well as 'natural-sounding'. Some would call this talent. It can be honed and developed, but I am not sure that everyone has a sustainable ability to act or that good acting can totally be taught. If it could, casting children would be much easier and it would hardly ever be necessary to look outside full-time stage schools.

ROUND 2

So far, most of the people we have seen have been on familiar territory (except the ones who came to an 'office audition'). The next step is to organise a rehearsal or conference room, and arrange for all those on the shortlist to meet us there. If possible, this will be on a Saturday or after school. This stage is intended to be more of a challenge. Everyone knows they are on a shortlist. Everyone is on new territory, meeting many strangers. There will often be at least four people to please including the executive producer. It may seem tough, but I reckon that if a child cannot cope with this still friendly challenge, then the stresses of location or studio working would also be too much. I have seen many children of whom I had had high hopes falter at this stage.

The form of this audition is slightly different from the first round. We may still ask for an improvisation, but this will be on a topic directly connected with the script. For the readings, the script will be a new scene. The big difference from the first audition is that people will be expected to read more than once and with different combinations of other children. This is important for two reasons. It gives us an idea of how a group in the script, that may be friends or siblings, look and sound together, and it gives the individuals a chance to meet and see if they can actually work together. We may be trying some children out in different parts, too.

In Children's Television Drama, it is common for children to have the major parts. The success or failure of an entire series may hang on how well we make our decisions about casting. If the first shortlist has been extensive, we may need to hold a further audition, known as a 'recall'. This may be inconvenient for the children concerned – but it is not half as bad as our choosing a child who cannot cope or who is wrong for the part. This audition is similar to the second but with fewer children. Feelings are high at this stage. By the end of this audition the Production Company should be able to make its decisions.

Some directors like to use a camcorder at auditions, so they have a fuller record of what they have seen.

Round 3 and beyond

Occasionally, particularly when there are several interested parties such as co-producers (other companies who may be providing part of the money for the production), yet another audition may be called. The problem is that, in the United Kingdom, it takes at least three weeks to process all the paperwork for a licence. Time may be running short, and if there is a problem in getting a licence for a particular child, there may be real difficulties in licensing a substitute.

It is very nice to be able to phone an agent – or a parent – and say, 'We have some good news – we want Jane (or Johnny) to play the leading rôle of Michaela (or Michael).' But it can be a different story. There are some auditions where you turn up at the beginning of the session with the rest of those who have been shortlisted. The people on the production then work with everyone, eliminating people one by one. It almost becomes a game like musical chairs. The longer you stay, the more you allow your hopes to build up, and the greater the disappointment when one of the team announces that you won't be required and you can go. I have run an audition like this but found it very painful to have to send boys and girls away, disappointed. George went to auditions like this for the 1990s' stage version of *Oliver*. He told me that they read off the names of people no longer required after each round. He felt lucky his name was not there each time, but as the auditions progressed tensions ran high. 'Everyone ends up really scared,' he said.

There are some children who find it is better to know where they stand as early as possible. If they are going to be rejected, most of those I have spoken to prefer a note in the post, although being told at the audition can help some simply to move on and get on with their lives.

Doing the right thing for everyone is difficult. What is clear is that ALL the people auditioned want to know definitely where they stand, they want to be told one way or the other by post or by phone.

Adele said, 'Some people just say. "We'll let you know." But you don't know WHEN they'll let you know. If you think you've done a good audition and you think you might have got the part when they, perhaps, really hated you, you're sitting here thinking, "Has anyone phoned?" And if there's a number on 1471 you don't recognise, you're thinking, "What? Missed it!" If you get down to the last three … they can let you know at the interview or on a different day. If they've narrowed it down to three, they should let you know if you've NOT got it, to give you some feedback. I just think it's best if they say, "We'll let you know by such and such date."'

The problem is that a lot of children – and adults – go for an interview or audition, and they hear nothing at all – unless they have got a part. All those I spoke to felt that those in at the final auditions ought to be told one way or another. 'It's frustrating after a week not to hear. If they say no, you can forget about it and think about the next one.'

Certainly, for those who go to a lot of auditions, the worst way to hear you have not got a part is that one of your friends has. Then again, there can be feelings of guilt if you get a part and the friend who went with you did not – it can be hard not to say the wrong thing.

Auditions can be tense both for actors and directors. We sometimes make mistakes or speak without thinking. Sebastian went to one audition in London for a film. 'There were three boys left. They told me I looked right for the part. It was, "Yes! Yes! – Except you'd be noticed from the programmes we did last year, so we can't have you."

'They said this in front of the other two boys. I was really embarrassed about it. I think if they're going to tell you something like that, they should tell you on your own.'

Nicola, who is at a full-time stage school, had some helpful thoughts. 'You're going to get a lot of knock-backs. The more auditions you go to, the more mistakes you'll make and the more you'll learn from your mistakes.'

Not getting a part doesn't necessarily mean making mistakes. It may simply come down to a feeling that the director will work more easily with one person than another. It may even be that one person looks more believable as part of a 'family group'.

The complexities are summed up by Adele. '[The Production is] narrowing it down. Then they turn round and say to people, "We can't have you for this part because you don't look right." But you see other people that don't match the rest of the family. They had in the lad who was to be playing my brother, and he's got brown hair. And they said to one of my friends who's got brown hair, "Can't have you 'cos you don't look right – you don't look like the family."

'Yet they kept a girl with bright ginger hair for the next round ... They took her to the read-through and the producer said, "No, she can't have that part because she doesn't look anything like the rest of the family."

'So they had to take that part away from her and give it to me. It's not very fair when that happens. I felt really bad. She must have felt awful, because she'd been shopping for her costume; she'd been to the read-through. Then they turned round and said, "You can't have the part!"'

In fact, Adele was over 16 when this happened to her, which is why she could take the part at such short notice. She did not have the licence to worry about. The story does show, though, that things can change at the last minute; that you have to please all the producers and the director as well as the casting director; the system can feel very unfair. It is very uncertain.

From the Production side, things are not always easy. During the casting process, I get to know – and like – most of the children. There is a strong feeling of regret about finally saying, 'No' to anyone, but, in the end, we must build the best possible cast. Sometimes we can offer smaller parts to those we have shortlisted. On the first series of *The Demon Headmaster* we needed around twenty 'children' to operate computers. There was quite a lot of acting needed even from those who did not have specific lines. I think it was quite a good experience for those we chose. Some were taken from the ranks of people we had auditioned for the main parts. In a later series, I was again able to offer a few days' work to several people who had come close to getting other major parts.

Personally, I find auditions nerve-wracking. I always want everybody to do well, and often regret that I haven't more parts on offer. There can be lighter moments though. Kristy Bruce has appeared in many shows apart from *The Demon Headmaster*. She remembers one occasion in particular, 'I went for an audition for *The Bill* when I was younger and I talked so much that the director said he would give me 20p AND the part if I stopped talking!'

I like this story – but on the whole, knowing when to shut up and listen is important!

Getting the part – or not

Obviously, it is great to be given the part you really worked for and wanted. But I wondered how it feels to be turned down, especially when you think you have done really well. Or what happens if you think you have done really badly and you get the part?

Lucas said, 'I came out of the audition. It was between me and two others. They thought it had gone well – they'd got loads of response from the director. Then the director called ME in. He shook my hand and said I'd got it!'

Charlotte thought she stood no chance at one audition. 'They had some really tall, skinny people. I thought, "They're going to get it." [Production people] were reeling off names; the numbers were whittled down. I was really shocked – but they wanted someone a bit shorter … (not better).'

George had been up for a Lynda la Plante project. 'I came out feeling so bad. The day after, they phoned and said I'd got it.'

Many felt the blow of being turned down was softened if it was done nicely, perhaps with a well-phrased letter. Certainly, for those at full-time stage school, if you do not get one part, it probably will not be long before another audition comes along and there will be the chance of another part. The positive side of doing a number of auditions – if you learn to cope with the rejections – is that you can build up your self-confidence and improve your interview technique.

George put this matter of dealing with rejections wisely. 'You learn to accept disappointments. You are in the business. It's going to happen. It's no good crying over it every time it happens. Get over it and just go for the next one.'

8 *Developing a Career*

What can child actors reasonably expect of child acting and what have they to look forward to if they try to continue as adults? After all, even though there are some performers who have been acting since they were children, most adult actors enter the profession as adults and most child actors change direction.

This is a difficult area. There is so much disappointment, so many broken dreams. There are so many good actors who haven't quite made it; they have real struggles to make ends meet. Only a small proportion of child actors carry on and do well. You do need something to fall back on!

So what's the difference?

To a large extent, acting for adults seems to be a different thing from acting for children. Mr Vote has been at the Italia Conti Academy long enough to see hundreds of 'his' children make the change. I asked him what he thought was the difference between child and adult acting. He said, 'Not much is expected of children. They are cast for the characteristics they have – to be themselves under the spotlight and in front of the cameras.'

I agree with this but would add that children have to be themselves whilst saying someone else's lines. They have to work hard and be adaptable, to fit in quickly with a team of professional people and they still have to do their schoolwork.

Mr Vote's view on adults is that they have to present 'multiple personalities'. From within themselves, they have to find and play Iago AND Othello, Bolingbroke AND Richard II and be equally convincing as 'both'. Even if different companies cast them in a succession of leading rôles, I would not expect children to change their performance to anything like the extent I would expect from most adults. This is not to say that some adult actors cannot succeed by giving the same performance again and again in different parts. The

American film star system was to some extent based on actors' abilities to do just this. Fifty years ago, you went to see a Cary Grant movie because you wanted to see Cary Grant – recognisably as himself (or as his screen *persona*).

Frances Amey was 10 when I gave her the part of Dinah in *The Demon Headmaster*. Her comment was, 'Children were given more direction on how to play the part and deliver lines, whereas adults were mostly left to interpret their parts in their own way.'

We can keep actors hard at it all day, but Frances said this difference shows up, too: 'Chaperones also made sure that the children had a break when they really needed one!'

The over-crowded profession

Most child actors and would-be child actors I have met have been told that acting is an over-crowded profession. Nonetheless, many want to go on and at least work in show business. This infatuation with the glamorous life may pass, it may be a phase. On the other hand, some children do seem to pick up an idea of what they want at a very early age – and stick to it.

There are many honest jobs in theatre, television and films, but long-term careers can no longer be guaranteed; acting itself is still a precarious profession. I think for children, taking part in a dramatic project can be a great experience. If you can cope at 10 or 12 with a professional television or film production – and not let it go to your head – then you learn a lot, quickly, about hard work, self-discipline and co-operation. It is also just about the best-paid work you are likely to get under the age of 16!

Many young actors recognise the problems. George said, 'Most child actors don't go on, they can get burnt out.' Some recognised the fact that adults trying to make a career as actors depend on their earnings; children do not. A child's earnings may be a contribution to the family economy, but it is rare for them to be so great that a family can live off them. This is partly because of the laws governing the number of days a child can work, and partly because the daily rate of pay is not high relative to average adult pay. There are also rules stating that a proportion of any fee must be paid into a savings account in the child's name, though it seems impossible to enforce a minimum limit on how long the money has to stay there …

Several children spoke of the way they were still totally dependent on their families. Charlotte said, 'Adults don't have as much choice.'

Andrew agreed: 'It's more fun for our age. It's more serious for adults.'

Unfair to kids?

Some children notice differences between the way they are treated and the way adults are treated. I was asked several times why children are paid less than adults are. On the face of it, it can seem unfair that the actor who comes in for two scenes may get a higher daily rate than the child who is in virtually every scene.

What these questioners had forgotten is that directors can work with children only for three-and-a-half hours a day. We must pay for a chaperone for them and provide a tutor during term time. We also have to provide either safe transport home or reasonable hotel accommodation. These are all significant costs that are not encountered with adult actors. Rates do vary a great deal for different jobs. One boy contrasted his pay of £100 an hour for some voice-over work he had done with the daily rate of £15 a day for other work, I guess that was in the theatre.

Some had other grounds for complaint, though. Lucas had found that sometimes the chaperone would 'talk down' to the children in her care. He'd also found a contrast between ordinary acting jobs and a radio play. There, the other actors had helped him, offering advice about what to do with his script and microphone technique. On other productions, he'd found that adults expected children 'just to get on with it'. Daniel, too, had felt more equally treated on a radio production, but had been in other situations where even child principals were not treated on equal terms with adults, but were 'put down'.

Lucas commented, 'Children won't complain. They're told, "It's a great experience." Adults do complain.'

Changing attitudes

It can be difficult to make the transition to being an adult actor in all sorts of ways. The point at which you cease to be a child is dependent on where your 16th birthday falls within the school year, so some individuals might be 16½ before we can stop providing tutors and chaperones. Also, the regulations are likely to change as law is standardised across Europe. Please bear this in mind in what follows.

When we began recording the Children's Drama, *The Demon Headmaster*, Gunnar Cauthery, who played Lloyd, was 14-years-old. By the time we were preparing the third series, he was just 16, and no longer needed either a tutor or a chaperone. Legally, we would have been quite within our rights to expect him to arrange his own transport and accommodation.

Of course, at 16, Gunnar was too young to drive, even if he'd had a car at his disposal. It all seemed rather unfair to me – especially as he was still at school, and about to start his 'A' level course. In the event, we arranged for him to stay at the hotel with the other 'children' as he had for the previous two series, and we made an exception and provided transport for him. It would have seemed irresponsible to me simply to throw him back on his own devices.

As well as his interest in acting, Gunnar is a keen musician, although all the professional work he has done has been simply acting. 'Now,' he says, 'I am quite difficult to pigeonhole, either as a "child" or as an "adult".' In the two years following *The Demon Headmaster*, he did not get any work despite attending as many auditions as ever. 'This,' he says, 'has forced me to analyse my approach to auditions and I feel less confident now than I used to. It feels as though I have got to prove myself over again.

'However, I have no regrets as regards my experience as a child actor because it has been my ardent ambition to pursue an acting career for as long as I can remember ... Had I discovered it was not to my liking, I could have ended my short career without much upheaval, and still in time to re-focus my education in pursuit of an alternative career.'

This age can be awkward. Adele, who had been dancing since she was 2 and appearing in local theatres, did not get her first major part on television until she was over 16. Her first part was that of a young teenager – one who would normally have needed tuition and chaperoning. 'Last year, because I was playing a child, I was treated as a child. They quite often thought that the chaperone who was there was my chaperone when she wasn't, so they treated me as a minor, really. But this year, on the second run, because I'm older, and I've got my own car that takes me there, they see me as being older. They seem to have a bit more respect – maybe because I'm with an adult cast. If the cast were mostly children, it might be different. In terms of a child with an adult cast, there's not so much respect – you get brushed aside.'

Not on my productions!

Like Adele, Jim is 18. He had had television work before he was 16, and is also building his experience as an adult actor.

'When I started,' he said, 'it was just good fun to have a part. As the years went by and I looked like being a professional, it was still fun and I still wanted to do things, but I want to do things a lot more. Parts that I got before, they just came to me …right place at the right time. Now, I have to go out and look for work – you know, try and keep yourself busy. Finding an agent in London was a problem. I've had a lot of help with it from parents and Central [now part of Carlton Television], but there's still a definite difference.'

He had been through the training at the Junior Television Workshop. I asked if he thought about any other training. 'I did a year at College, but I've just got an agent.'

Cath is 13 and had listened to all this. 'I haven't had a part yet, but I've been to auditions. They're exciting. But when you're an adult, I think you'd think, "Well, it's just another audition. It's not exciting really."'

Jim disagreed. 'I think it is exciting … It's more serious.'

Adele confirmed this, ' If you don't get the work, then you don't get any money. So you've got to get out there and get it.'

I asked about the different demands directors make as their actors get older.

Adele spoke again. 'I think as you get older, you tend to discuss things more. I mean this year I tend to discuss things with the director. Whereas with the lad it's, "Can you do this for me; can you do that?" Because he's younger, he's being told what to do. As you get older, you get more experience – with life, not just with working – then you know more what your reaction's going to be.'

I would certainly expect older actors to be able to offer a wider range of reactions and more ways to say some of their lines. This must lead to more discussion between actor and director.

Jim told me, 'I definitely needed a lot more direction than the older actors. The older people have probably got more skill to listen whereas, when you're younger, you're not quite as deep … As you get older, actors are cast more away from their own personality. They need to talk about their rôles.'

Some adult actors find it difficult working with children. I was watching a tape recently that kept running between takes. The scene was between an adult and a boy of 12. It was clear that the actor was concentrating all the time, between takes as well as during the performance. The boy was not concentrating. He was concerned about how his hair looked* and about everything that was happening in the studio. The result was that we had to record three or four takes because he kept forgetting his lines. Many children seem able to laugh and joke and then to turn on their performance at a moment's notice. This can be difficult for all but the most experienced and able adults.

It is interesting that the experience of the young people I spoke to does tally with what I had expected. Mind you, I did have the doubtful pleasure of working with one busy 17-year-old. She came back to my rehearsals from a short engagement on an adult drama. She spoke very disparagingly of the adult actors – especially those playing small parts – who were concerned about their motivation and the background of their respective characters. 'Why can't they just get on with it and do it?' she asked the world at large. I had had some difficulty in persuading her to rehearse to my satisfaction. Maybe she should remember the old quotation, 'There are no small parts, only small actors!' 1999 was, after all, the year when Judi Dench won an Oscar for a small part in the film *Shakespeare in Love*.

Unchanging attitudes

If we have the chance to employ someone just over licensing age to play someone under licensing age, that does make life a lot easier for us. This is what Adele had done – played down, that is, played younger. Some actors seem able to carry on looking very young for years. It can become irksome in your mid-twenties – or older – still to be playing adolescents. In practice, it is more likely that stage actors will have more extreme versions of this problem than screen actors. The closer the cameras, the harder it is to conceal your age. I remember a stage version of *Peter Pan* where all the lost boys were aged about 20! This could not have happened on screen.

Making the change – comments from Anna Scher

Anna Scher has seen many child actors come and go. Some have stayed in the profession and done very well as actors, some have moved into production. All began at ordinary schools (as opposed to stage schools.) Actors she has taught include Linda Robson and Pauline Quirke, popular together in the tv series *Birds of a Feather*,

---

* This was not vanity – he was concerned about continuity (see chapter 13).

Susan Tully, who became a leading actor first in *Grange Hill* then in the BBC soap-opera, *Eastenders*; and the brothers Mark and Ray Burdis, Mark appearing in *Grange Hill* and Ray having had starring rôles on tv.

Many of the main characters in *Grange Hill* began their acting with Anna. Her theatre continues to be an important fountainhead in the supply of child actors. I found Frances Amey there, at 10-years-old, she had just joined the theatre and had never even auditioned before I met her and put into the leading rôle of Dinah in *The Demon Headmaster*.

Talent and luck

We talked about 'making the change' and the differences in demand on adults and children. What is clear is that Anna's view of child actors is unique in the UK and her influence has been huge. Her main interest and focus are still centred in the teaching that she does. She has not allowed herself to become diverted merely into 'running the business'.

'Because all the people here are so grounded in reality and we have none of the 'star status' nonsense, the transition can be seamless in many ways, particularly if they come to class.'

Her classes cover voice modulation, projection and diction, eye contact and the other communication skills. She runs classes for young professionals and professionals as well as for children.

Talking about becoming an adult actor, she said, 'It's a fact that 85% of actors are out of work at any one time. It's an over-crowded profession. You must have a second string. You could be Judi Dench and you could be out of work. And who wants to depend on Lady Luck?

'It's to do with talent, persistence, perseverance and tenacity … But one has to be realistic without destroying the dream … We have a fantastically good batting average because so many people [casting directors and the like] do come down here, as it were automatically. Having said that … you must have that second string to your bow. Get yourself properly qualified to teach – get skills like driving, typing. You've just got to because lots of people want to act and it can be hugely disappointing. There's lots of rejection … You have to have a tremendously strong core … At the end of the day, there are other things as well. There are alternatives to acting professionally …'

The voice

Children who gain acting experience and begin to think of acting as a career, sooner or later run into the question of accent. In auditions, we look for actors who we think will be convincing in the rôles they play. One part of this is how they sound. This is partly to do with the way they say lines and it is partly to do with accent. We all have an accent. Some people have several. Some young people have one they use at home and one they slip into at school.

How important is it for an adult actor to be able to use several accents? Is it a good idea to try and lose a regional accent and learn Received Pronunciation?

There was a time when stage and drama schools made a big point of teaching 'correct' pronunciation, and of 'ironing-out' regional accents. Those times are long gone and there is now an emphasis on 'being yourself'. Adult actors will obviously widen the range of parts they can play if they speak with Received Pronunciation AS WELL AS their own natural accent. Not all actors even try and do this. Some do very well through having a distinctive voice that they use for all acting purposes. There is no one-and-only way. I think the best advice is to avoid doing anything that feels false. Not every actor has the talent for mimicry of Peter Ustinov or Rory Bremner.

I asked Anna Scher about this. She said, 'We teach RP as one would a dialect, like an American dialect. We don't teach it in an elocution-like way.'

I asked if actors might be limiting themselves simply by having only their original accent. 'It's a good point, yes … Most parts are written in Standard English. Therefore any actor should have Standard English. It's really a requirement unless you want to end up playing Irish maids for the rest of your life.'

Anna agreed that it gives more flexibility and more range. 'It must. That's being sensible.'

The agency

Agents – for adults and children – attached to the Anna Scher Theatre have a five-point rôle. They should:

- communicate clearly – and that's a two-way thing – actors can get so poisonous about their agents. There's got to be mutually effective communication.

- be supportive
- promote their clients
- negotiate fees and contracts
- work on career development.

The emphasis is on skills, not looks. People are encouraged to be professional. There are five Ps: Punctuality, Preparation, Presentation, Practice, Positive. These attitudes are expected, for standards are as important as talent.

Life beyond acting

With Anna's emphasis on communication skills, it struck me that students who don't want to go into the acting profession should do well in other walks of life. She agreed, commenting that the acting experience had often given students the confidence to go into nursing or teaching or social work, or had made them more effective parents. She added: 'I always talk about "confidence, not cockiness". There's another fine line!'

On the other hand

I think drama taught as Anna teaches it would probably help many to be 'confident, not cocky'. And there are many drama teachers up and down the country who can give all their students more confidence in communication.

If you were to watch group improvisations under Anna's guidance, you would probably be struck by the high levels of aggression. This enables children to work out conflicts in their lives through drama and to resolve some of their inner conflicts. I have met a very few youngsters from the AST who gave me the impression that they could have been difficult, especially in some dark alley. Working with these individuals, on the other hand, has been a delight. Whatever their home difficulties and problems, 'on set' they have been able, hard-working and polite.

Generally, an energy may be needed to make a scene interesting. Because many improvisations look at aggression, 'aggressive' is often an easy way to play a scene. That is fine. But on location, it is easy for a director and child actor to perform many scenes like this, almost without realising it. When the scenes are placed end to end, you are left with a show in which the cast seem to be more hostile to each other than the script demands, and the world view becomes unnecessarily pessimistic. It is the director's job to prevent this.

Cautionary tales and 'child stars'

I have already mentioned that Anna Scher thinks it is dangerous to call any child a 'star'. Remembering that we had first met in the early days of *Grange Hill*, Anna said, 'Something that has concerned me is the phrase "*Grange Hill* star". They are *Grange Hill* actors … There are child actors as there are child swimmers, child tennis-players … Often I'm asked to do a phone-in programme on the acting business. If they say, "child star-maker, Anna Scher," I immediately take the interviewer to task … It's a daft word. Success needs to be earned.'

In fairness to those I know who have been involved with *Grange Hill*, I think the linking of the word 'star' with the series has usually come from outside the *Grange Hill* unit. Most frequently it seems to have stemmed from the publicity machine that works within the BBC, and over which the programme makers have had far less control than is sensible. Nonetheless, the general point Anna makes is serious.

Child actors may take a prominent place in millions of homes up and down the land for a few weeks, but they then have to go back to school, to pick up where they were before they were 'famous'. It may be that this is easier in a full-time stage school than in the average comprehensive. Everybody concerned is used to the phenomenon, for a start. On the other hand, children at ordinary schools may gain considerably in confidence and in their ability to concentrate and work hard.

Some children go on to normal careers, some pick up more and more work in 'the business', and become professional actors. There are a few for whom the experience of child acting turns sour, maybe as a result of unrealistic expectations being placed on them, maybe for lack of the right kind of support and guidance.

As I write, Bonnie Langford is starring in a West End musical, playing the title rôle in *Sweet Charity*. She began her acting career very young and went to the Italia Conti Academy. Many people in the UK still remember her in, for instance, the 1970s' television adaptation of Richmal Crompton's *William* books. She has been eminently successful in making the transfer to adult acting. Everything I have heard or read about her confirms that she has worked hard and consistently to achieve this – continuous success in any job can only be achieved by application and hard work.

On the other hand, Macaulay Culkin became famous on both sides of the Atlantic following his appearances in *Home Alone*, and its sequels. According to an article by Patricia Driscoll in *The Sunday Times* of 28 June 1998, '... his marriage last week ... was dismissed in certain circles as a giant publicity stunt. One commentator observed tartly: "The industry regards him as a has-been."

'Let me run that by you again: Culkin, once the hottest star in the Hollywood firmament, is a has-been. At 17.'

The article also referred to his parents' legal battle '... to control him – and his move to 'divorce' his father.'

Fortunately, these are extreme cases.

I think it is fair to say that the supervision in the UK is sufficient to keep most children out of trouble most of the time. Hours are exceeded, and children may be somewhat overworked from time to time and their schoolwork may suffer, but I have not heard of working under-16s getting into trouble with drink, drugs or sex.

Once they move beyond the protection of the law for under-16s, the dangers can begin. Former child actors have been mentioned to me as drug-takers and alcoholics. Most worrying are rumours of the occasional young actor who has acted on set while 'under the influence'. I cannot in any way condone this sort of behaviour. The Production has no control here, unless they terminate the actor's contract. I am not suggesting that smoking, excessive drinking of alcohol and involvement with drugs are more widespread among young actors than among the population at large. It is just that young actors can be in the position of having access to earnings relatively large for their age, and that some kind of labelling as a 'star' might make a heady combination that will drive out common sense and distort the judgement.

Ambitions

I suppose most girls who manage to persuade their parents to get them their own pony have some vague ambition – however fleeting – to be international show jumpers. Do all child actors have ambitions to be international film stars? Certainly, most will not realise that dream. If they cannot fulfil one dream, they may be forced or may choose to find another career. But then I know many people who fell into their present careers almost by accident. Many of these changed their minds about what they wanted as adults years after leaving school. At 15, for instance, I thought I wanted to become a doctor. It was only at medical school that I became deeply involved with the 'wrong' kind of theatre.

I met one former child actor (who had been to one of the London full-time stage schools) when he came to survey the dry rot under my floor. He had done a fair amount of acting work as a boy but it all gradually dried up, and he realised he needed to build another career. He is good at his job and he speaks happily of his days at the Barbara Speake School in West London.

Mr Vote told me some ex-pupils of Conti's have gone on to teaching – one he recalls went on to be a barrister. Of those that stay in 'the business', he said, 'The reality of life is that most of our children are not going to be brain surgeons ... They will have average jobs and lead very interesting lives.' Nonetheless, he claims a high degree of success for the Italia Conti Academy in starting students on their careers. He has seen people take their first jobs on *Eastenders* and *Hollyoaks*. Others leave to become mainstream actors and show-dancers. Other ex-Conti students include Noel Coward, Leslie Phillips and Tracey Ullman.

'Our goal is to make the business accessible,' said Mr Vote. Inevitably, there is not enough work all the year round for all the dancers in, for instance, Blackpool, but the Academy overall, he says, has one of the highest proportions of ex-students who stay in the business.

Some child actors move into production. John Howard-Davies is widely remembered by my generation for his film portrayals of Pip in *Great Expectations* and Tom in *Tom Brown's Schooldays*. He was for years on the staff of the BBC as a highly successful tv producer in Light Entertainment and his more recent credits include *The Vicar of Dibley*. Ray Burdis was one of the earlier members of the Anna Scher Theatre and has taken leading television rôles as an adult. He now works as a producer. Even among my own former colleagues in the Children's Drama Unit at the BBC there were two who had worked as child actors. One was Paul Stone, who produced, among other series, *The Box of Delights* directed by Renny Rye, and *The Chronicles of Narnia*. The other was Marilyn Fox, who directed *The Lion, the Witch and the Wardrobe*. Her career began on the radio in Northern Ireland when she was 12. Her directing credits include *Five Children and It*, *The Return of the Psammead* and *Earthfasts*, in which she cast as co-lead Paul Nicholls who has since played major parts in series like *City Central* and *Eastenders*.

Eastenders, of course, has taken on a number of actors who began working as children – especially on *Grange Hill*. Todd Carty, who plays Mark in *Eastenders* and already had an impressive list of credits when he began playing Tucker in the first series of *Grange Hill*. Susan Tully joined *Grange Hill* later and was an original member of the cast of *Eastenders*. Since she left that series, she has continued to develop her career.

Many child actors continue doing a little work here and there. Some give up or move on. At least one of the early 'leading lights' of *Grange Hill* has become a hairdresser. (The model Naomi Campbell also started on *Grange Hill*, as an 'extra'.) Other child actors have told me they do not want to stay in the business. They have chosen to go back to 'normal' schools and to take GCSEs and 'A' levels, and perhaps to seek further qualifications for more normal careers.

Hard choices

Thirty years on

For some, the choices can be hard. I know myself that, before I diverted into medicine, I had always wanted to work in theatre or television. In those days, there were not the courses or university opportunities that there are now.

When I was asked at school about university choices and 'A' level preferences, it was hard for me to stick to the idea of getting a job in the theatre or at the BBC. We had no connections in the business, no-one to advise us, no-one to talk to. In the event, I was nudged into science 'A' levels and a course in medicine at University College London. I dropped out of that course. My heart was not in it. It did not help that my surviving parent died at the end of my first year. It was in the aftermath of all this, working for a living and deciding where I really wanted my future to lie that I wrote to the BBC and asked for a job. It was different in those days. They gave me one.

My time at University College was not wasted. I learnt a great deal about the practice of theatre while I was there, and several students moved into television and theatrical careers, some of us without gaining any further qualification. I have noticed that a great proportion of my friends have changed their minds about their careers after leaving school 'certain' about what they wanted to do.

Choosing a career is hard. Contracts that last until you are 60, which the BBC used to offer, are things of the past.

The trick is to leave some options open, leaving you room for manoeuvre. The easiest way of doing this is to get qualifications while you can – and to accumulate marketable skills. Computer, keyboard and driving skills are always useful.

A younger view

I spoke to an 18-year-old who is thinking hard about the future. 'I've had all these plans to get an education first, go to university. When I've done that, at least then, if acting doesn't work out, then I've got something to fall back on …

'A lot of actors that I've spoken to have said, "Get an education – there's no age limit on acting." But the more I do it, the more I want to do it and the less appealing is going to university.'

My own view is this. If you have been offered a place on a course you want at a good university, and can afford it, take it. It will not stop you going back to acting and it might well give you a broader perspective on life. On the other hand, do investigate and choose the course you are thinking about carefully. It is all too easy to get on a course that sounds great but is disappointing six months in!

Perhaps the biggest problem about acting as a child – or at least whilst still at school – is the distraction that paid work puts in the way of schoolwork. If this teenager, for instance, had not taken work when she was 17, would she be feeling any doubts now about university? I doubt it. Perhaps children should not be allowed to act at all – then, perhaps, there would be no problem!

On the other hand, the teenager says herself, 'Kids like to watch kids of their own age relate to things. If you don't do any acting until you're 21, then you're not going to have the experience, you're not going to know what to do … When you're a child, if you're doing something that your friends haven't done, it's great. It's great to experience things that no-one else has done.'

At 14, Andrew's view about child acting is very positive. 'If you think you should wait until you're 21, by all means wait until 21. But if not, go ahead. If it doesn't work, then that's a mistake you've made … It's best to make your mistakes while you're young – then you've got time to catch up.'

9 Between 'Getting the Part' and Rehearsal

Let us suppose you've got the part. What next? This chapter will attempt to answer that question. Most of what follows deals with the events leading up to a drama project on television. Commercials are often shot in only a couple of days, so some steps may not be necessary. Films will be organised slightly differently and may not bother with rehearsals. Stage plays are likely to have longer in rehearsal and a lower overall budget. If they have a long run planned, they may have two or three 'teams' of children playing in different performances.

The first step …

… is to start the booking process. This is in two parts.

First, there has to be an agreement between the Production Company, the agent (if there is one) and the child – and his or her legal guardian. This agreement will cover the number of working days, when those days are and the fees involved. It will also define any rehearsal days and what happens about costume and make-up calls. There will probably be a lot of detail, which is why it can be so helpful to have an agent who knows what is normal and reasonable.

In television, this contract also defines what happens if the programme is repeated, sold to other companies based abroad and what happens if it is released on video cassette. Lots of paperwork is needed to keep track of everybody. The fees for a showing in a small country might be less than the cost of issuing a cheque. It is increasingly likely, therefore, that most people entitled to these 'residual payments' will be offered a 'buy-out'. This is a single payment offered in advance of any sales to cover all such possibilities. The advantage is that you get a little more money up front and that you might have got nothing if the project did not sell. The disadvantage is that you may lose out if the project becomes immensely successful and sells to, say, the United States networks and German networks. This is all so perplexing that you really do need advice.

It sounds complicated, and it is, but it may be helpful to realise that many of the clauses in the contract will be fairly standard. Also there will probably not be much difference between contracts for children working on the same project or for children working on different projects for the same company.

The second part for those under school-leaving age is the licence. This is VERY important, and complicated, and is dealt with in chapter 5. This is just a reminder that, for those under school-leaving age, it is not possible to work in this country on professional stage, film or television productions without a licence. A licence usually takes at least three weeks to arrange, so the process should be under way three weeks before the first performance day. Ideally it should be under way three weeks before the first rehearsal day. If anything goes wrong, the Production will have to recast. If this happens because a licence is refused, the contract ceases to be effective. Everyone concerned needs to fill in his or her section of the forms as fully, accurately and quickly as possible.

Reams of paper

After the auditions and the flurry of paperwork concerning the licence, things probably go quiet for a little while. It used to be normal in BBC Children's Drama for a letter to be sent to parents and child actors outlining, simply, what was going on and emphasising that:

- accepting the offer was a professional commitment and had to be completed unless there was an illness or injury;
- the Production would pay for and provide a tutor (where necessary);
- the Production would pay for and provide a chaperone;
- there were clear start and finish dates;
- there would be information and requests coming from the Production, the costume designer and the make-up designer.

We would sometimes send some of this information through just before the final audition, so that those new to the business would have a clearer idea of what they were letting themselves in for. In particular, it is important to remember that contracts are binding.

The order in which things happen now varies, but quite a lot more paper is likely to arrive through the letterbox – sometimes even by courier, if time is short.

Scripts

Usually we send all the complete scripts involving each child's character. This is so that it is easy to see how each actor's scenes fit into the story. It also clarifies the overall tone of the story. If you have a big part in a series or serial, it can look daunting – it is easy to feel that you could never learn all that! Well, in a film or tv series, you never have to perform everything in one go. This is where the schedule is important – but I'll come back to that later.

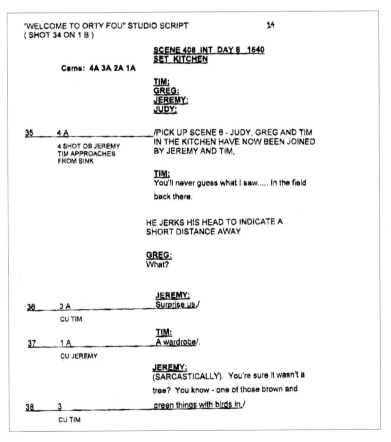

Welcome to orty-Fou, a page of camera script. I added camera details during rehearsal. These show shot and camera numbers, camera position etc.

Each script is clipped together securely before it leaves the office. Sometimes, these clips work loose, resulting in the script fluttering over the floor in pieces. Some actors put each script into a folder that holds them more firmly. Most actors go through their scripts highlighting their names at the beginning of each of their speeches – sometimes they highlight the whole of each speech. This is a good idea – it helps you see how much you have to do, and it helps ensure you do not skip any lines. If anything is unclear, or not understood, a pencil mark next to that bit of the script will help you find the place when you get the chance to discuss it.

It is a good idea to go through the scripts to get a clear idea of the story, of your character and how you fit in. It is not necessarily a good idea to start learning individual speeches yet – unless you have specifically been told otherwise and time is very short!

When you do come to learn your scenes, it is no good merely learning your lines. You have to know how they fit the scene. You have to know whose lines your lines follow and what your cue is. One boy I knew was lazy about learning his script. If he learnt anything, it was only his speeches. The result was that, if there were a dramatic pause – any pause at all, he would come out with one of his lines. His lines were therefore in the wrong place and sometimes he did not even get them in the right order. This was very annoying for everybody – including me. Even my patience, which is considerable with actors, wore thin! He had been acting for years before I met him, so he had no real excuse, just plenty he made up on the spur of the moment, like, 'I didn't know we were doing this scene today.'

To which we would reply, 'It's in the schedule!'

And his answer to that was, 'But I've lost my schedule!'

Actually, a lot of actors say they have lost scripts or schedules, or have never received them, which is why my assistants now keep a logbook of which versions of which paperwork they have sent out on any particular day. If you say you have not received something, given that the Post Office is generally reliable, it suggests that one of the production team has not been doing the job properly and could get into trouble. It is also not very clever to say that you have not got a schedule on Tuesday, when everyone remembers your doodling on it last Friday!

If you have made a mistake, it is far better to say, 'Sorry, it's my fault, I forgot,' than to lie. Best, of course, is to keep yourself organised like a truly professional actor and to know exactly where your papers are.

Schedules

If the whole production, or even a substantial part of it, is to be shot on single camera, and if it will take more than a few days, you will almost certainly receive a schedule. This document is very important because it is all about communication. What information will be there, and how it is laid out, will, naturally, vary from one production to another. I will take as an example the one we used on the final series of *The Demon Headmaster*. The main responsibility for the content and the layout of the schedule belonged to my Production Manager, Claire. The other main contributor on my production was Alison, my Production Assistant. (On some productions, Claire

THURSDAY 31ST JULY	**SHOOTING DAY:** FIFTEEN
	SUNRISE: 5.15 **SUNSET:** 20.58
UNIT CALL: 0900 (Breakfast available from 0800)	**APPROX WRAP:** 1800
UNIT BASE:	Rose Gardens Council Offices Car Park See Map J
LOCATION:	RICKMANSWORTH HIGH STREET (Various) Herts
CONTACT:	Peter Brooker, Three Rivers District Council
DIRECTIONS:	See Directions 10, Maps I, J and K
PARKING:	In Unit Base as above
TO SHOOT SCENES:	208, 208A, 632, 633A, 645, 631
ARTISTS:	DEMON HEADMASTER Terrence Hardiman DINAH HUNTER Frances Amey LLOYD HUNTER Gunnar Cauthery HARVEY HUNTER Thomas Szekeres MANDY Rachael Goodyer INGRID Kristy Bruce MICHAEL DEXTER Jay Barrymore SMITH Tony Osoba
ARTIST CALLS & TRANSPORT:	Please see CAROLINE CALEY
CHAPERONES:	SUE SUMMERSKILL BERNADETTE KELLY BARBARA BRYAN (Birmingham)
SUPPORTING ARTISTS:	Bus Driver Supporting artists x 4 Kids x 4
SPECIAL NOTES:	Police x 1 on location UNIT BASE MOVE ON WRAP
LOCATION LOOS:	Mobile loos at unit base
CATERING NUMBER TODAY:	58

Schedule

might have been called the First Assistant. Job titles change but there will be somebody looking after each function I mention – whatever they call themselves!)

Schedules can be lengthy. You do not need to read every word, but it is important, and it shows how much thought and planning go into a production – especially one working on location.

- There should be an index to help you find your way around.
- There will be a staff list, naming practically everyone on the crew that you are likely to meet, and some you may not, such as the videotape editors.
- There will be a full cast list of all the characters involved in the shoot, and the names of all the actors whose contracts have been confirmed. There will probably also be a list of agents involved, and perhaps the local education authorities of each child.
- There will be a list of useful contact numbers; there should be one particular person whose main job is to look after the actors. This may be a Second or Third Assistant, a Stage Manager or in the BBC an AFM (Assistant Floor Manager), a Floor Assistant (in ITV some companies call them AFMs) or a Runner.
- There could be a chart showing all the days that individual actors (including children) are needed. Of course, if there are problems, there may have to be alterations.
- If any of the cast have to stay away from home, the Production will arrange hotels. There should be information about those details.
- A good schedule will list numbers for hospitals, doctors, dentists, police stations, banks and so on in the area of the location. Named doctors will have been warned about the production, and will be aware that their services could on occasion be needed.
- We usually include a summary of the hours permitted for children.
- The location caterers will be named. If there are no location caterers, there should be details of the catering arrangements.
- There will be maps and written travel directions to each location from some convenient central point and from the hotels (if any).
- **Last and most importantly, there will be the daily call sheets. These are so important that I shall go into more detail.**

The following points should be quite clear from the daily call sheet.

1 The *Day of the Month* that the sheet refers to.
2 The *Unit Call* This is the time at which everybody concerned in

the first scene of the day is expected to be ready to look at the action for the first shot.

3 The *Wrap* This is the time at the end of the day when production will finish and release the camera crew. The actors may be needed right up to the Wrap, but sometimes there are odd shots of things that may not need actors. Sometimes the design crew may have to stay on, clearing up or preparing things for the next day.

4 *Unit Base* This may be a film stage, as at Pinewood or Shepperton, or it may be a location. If there is limited space at the location, the base might be a nearby community centre or school. It is the place where everyone meets for the day, where the location caterers (if any) will set up, where Costume and Make-up are based and where all non-essential vehicles are parked. Parking looms large in the life of people like Claire, and careful – and strict – arrangements are always made.

5 *Location* This may or may not be at the Unit Base. The word means either the 'story' location or the real location, or both. So in *The Demon Headmaster* second series, we had a location called in the script 'The Biogenetic Research Centre'. For this, we used an old stately home called 'The Vache'. When we were there, we called it 'The Vache' or 'The BRC' as the fancy took us. In either case it was 'the Location'.

6 *Contacts* These are the people responsible for the Unit Base and the Location. They could be a churchwarden, if the Unit Base were a church hall, and a local police sergeant, if the location were the street just outside the hall.

7 *Scenes* There will always be a list of scenes that are planned for the day.

8 *Artists* There will always be a list of actors who will be needed in those scenes.

9 *Artists' Calls* These may be listed in the schedule or they may be given individually by the Third Assistant or whoever is looking after the actors. This person will give a time for each actor to arrive at the Unit Base, and go to Make-up or Costume. If there are children involved, there will also be arrangements about transport.

10 The *chaperones* and tutors who are needed will be listed.

11 *Supporting Artists* will be listed. These are usually non-speaking 'background artists' who make the place look as busy as necessary. In some circumstances, they used to be called 'extras'. Because we are unlikely to know all the individual names by the time the

schedule is printed, the supporting artists are likely to appear listed like this: 10 bus passengers, 5 male, 5 female; 1 bus driver; 6 passers-by, 3 male, 3 female; 1 uniformed police constable. And so on.

12 There may well be information about lavatories.

13 Any special information about, perhaps, helicopters or special effects will be included.

14 **We always include a 'breakdown' of the scenes to be shot. This gives:**
   - **the episode and scene number**
   - **the page number in the original script**
   - **the cast needed**
   - **the location**
   - **brief details of that part of the story**
   - **the *Story Day*. This is an indication of where the scene is in relation to the whole story.** One episode might take place just on one day, but another might involve several days, and time passing. Episode 1 might be set, for instance, entirely on Monday. Episode 2 might start on Friday, jump to Sunday then to a Monday a year later. These would be Story Days 1, 2, 3 and 4. It is helpful to think like this for costume, for instance.

The schedule is important because it can answer most of the daily questions that you may ask! It is important that you know which scenes you are in each day, and it is important to know the lines for *those* scenes! It is also a good idea to know what is due to happen over the following few days. If the schedule does change, you are less likely to be taken by surprise.

Scheduling problems

Of course, a production may take several weeks to shoot. The schedule is often published before shooting begins and a lot can happen to upset these plans. It may become necessary to reschedule a day or even a few days. If this happens, then new pages may be issued for the affected days. If you are given new sheets, look after them and check what they mean to you! It is totally unprofessional to turn up for shooting having learnt the wrong script '… because I lost my schedule' or '… because nobody told me.' This second excuse will hardly ever be true.

What can happen to make things go wrong?

The weather is the most uncertain factor. If it rains, it can be very difficult to keep on shooting outside. I have known really heavy rain stop shooting indoors, too, when the noise of the rain on a roof made the sound recordist's job impossible. Another problem might be the illness of one of the principal members of the cast. We would expect actors to keep going with minor ailments, but I have sent home one child with bronchitis (knowing there was somebody there to look after him) and another to hospital with appendicitis. In the first case, we had to reschedule only a couple of days, in the other, on *Grange Hill*, we had to rewrite an entire script.

The other director of that series of *Grange Hill* was taken ill as well, and this caused major problems, too. He became sick the day before staging the School Musical. I had to pick up what he had planned and try to make it work.

Costume and make-up

It is quite possible that anyone playing a character with complicated hair, make-up or costume requirements will have a call from the make-up and costume designers before rehearsals start. It may be necessary to arrange a meeting, or even a shopping expedition and a wig fitting. It there is a rehearsal period, these things can sometimes be done then. If the meeting has to be outside the contracted time, then there should be a small fee payable for your time. Any such arrangement should be organised to avoid disruption of schoolwork.

Generally, these meetings are straightforward. The designers I work with know their job, and know what the director wants for each character. If the piece has a period setting, then you must trust the designers completely. If the piece is modern, then you should still trust the designers.

Costumes

Films, television drama and commercials are not dealing with reality: they are dealing with an image of reality. That image may be enhanced or exaggerated to make something clear. It does not matter that you would not be seen dead in a particular label or with a particular haircut. It is what suits the character that is important. Rachael Goodyer, who played Mandy in *The Demon Headmaster* says, 'I get annoyed when people comment on "my strange dress sense" when they see my clothes on tv. I would just like to say that most of the time, actors do not choose what they wear and Costume chooses

Costume –Tom Szekeres on location
in *The Demon Headmaster*

clothes that suit the tv character. Pink dungarees aren't my style!'

Sometimes, a designer will ask a child's opinion about current fashion, and may use the response in calculating the final 'look'. Certainly, there is no good reason for anyone to wear clothes that are really uncomfortable (unless that is the point of them), or that are skimpy beyond the bounds of fashion.

Adele has had bad and good experiences. On the first major part she had, there was no consultation. The woman said, 'This is what you're wearing.' I thought it was tat. I thought it didn't suit my character. It made me look about 13 or 14. I was supposed to be 17 ...

'Because it was my first part, I didn't dare say anything ... And then [on the second series], we got a different bloke who took me shopping, saying, "What do you think she'd wear for this?"

'Because I was given the opportunity to say, "I think she'd wear this," "I think she'd wear that," – like, we'd discussed it and come to an agreement – I felt more part of it and more part of the character. I think it helps you get into the character when you've discussed the costume.'

I suggested that if the piece had been set in, say, the 1950s, young actors would be more inclined to accept the costume designer's opinion. Adele agreed. 'I'd trust their judgement because that's their job.'

Seb joined in. 'I'd just got to the Workshop and I got my first part two weeks later. I thought, "I'll wear what they want me to wear." If they'd put red jeans on me, I'd have worn them!'

This was in a modern piece. 'In fact the clothes they gave me to wear were OK, though I wouldn't have worn them . . . '

I asked him if he thought the character would wear those clothes.

'Yeah, probably. I wouldn't argue with them, but if they asked for my opinion, I'd tell them what I thought the character would wear.'

The second series of *Grange Hill* took about seven months to shoot. It was the first time that BBC Children's Programmes had made such a long drama series and we ran into difficulties on several counts. Things changed greatly in later years, but in 1978, we filmed the location shots over the summer in and around Kingsbury in North London. This included scenes in the Kingsbury school hall, the dining areas, some corridors, the playgrounds and the playing fields. Scenes in homes, a classroom and the headmaster's offices were recorded at the BBC Television Centre in a multi-camera studio. This meant that some scenes from the later episodes were recorded in July and some in the following January.

Naturally, children grow. There are times when they grow quite fast. You can imagine the sort of difficulty that can occur. In one scene, Tucker may be shorter than the Art Mistress, and in the next, the same height. Todd Carty played the character Tucker, and I remember that his character's shoes, which had fitted perfectly in the summer, were too small for him by the time we were approaching the end of the series. The costume designer was very efficient and good at his job, but he had not calculated for this problem. He could not find a larger pair of shoes in the same style and Todd had to suffer for his art.

Two students at Italia Conti's had had a really uncomfortable day wearing 1970s' costumes. These had all been fitted from measurements, which had been phoned or faxed through. And nobody's costume fitted. 'It was horrible – a really hot day,' said one of the victims.

Tom Szekeres commented that, 'Old-fashioned clothes often present problems, especially the button-fly and tights(!)'

Tom Brodie enjoyed costume fittings, for which there is often a small extra payment. 'Money for old rope. I found it a great opportunity to go shopping in London, getting to know your costume designer.'

Make-up

On the whole, make-up seems to be less of a problem. In a modern piece, and with modern cameras, so far as children are concerned the less make-up, the better. One of the main areas of consideration is hair. If a character is appearing in a long series, and if that series is being shot out of story order, each character's hair will probably need frequent small trims just to keep the style constant. Obviously, for some scenes it might need to be tidy and for others, wind-blown, for instance. But there will not be any shocks when different scenes are put together, with hair suddenly growing, then shortening again.

One girl told me she does have a problem with make-up. 'It always poses a problem when I tell the make-up artists I am allergic to most make-up, especially stage make-up.'

If you know of any skin allergies you owe it to yourself and everybody else to let the make-up artist know! Serious problems are uncommon, but occasional allergic reactions to different elements of make-up can crop up. Spirit gum upsets several actors I know.

Anyone appearing in a costume drama may need to wear a wig. This applies especially to girls, but boys, too, will need long hair for some periods of history, as recent as the 1970s. Some wigs are available from the stock of wig suppliers; others may have to be made. In my experience, wherever possible, the make-up designer would avoid putting children into wigs and would try to use only a hairpiece. These may be harder to blend in to real hair, but they are less liable to come unstuck and to need the attention that a full wig demands.

In *The Story of the Treasure Seekers* two of the six Bastable children are girls. Fortunately, both the girls we chose in 1981 had long hair. We did not need to find wigs for them. One or two scenes were set at night, at bedtime. Around 1900, when the book was written, girls would go to great lengths to keep their hair curly, and would spend a long time each evening putting their hair into curl-papers or curl-

Frances Amey in make-up,

rags. In order to give the right feel to the piece, the younger character, Alice, had to have her hair put into these curl-rags several times.
It would have taken an hour or more. We did not have the time and
compromised, putting in about half the proper number of rags. This
took long enough, but the result was better than if we had not
bothered at all.

SPECIAL EFFECTS

Occasionally, life can be a little uncomfortable. If there are some
special effects needed, perhaps to show medical conditions or
injuries, it may be necessary for the make-up designer to take a cast
of all or part of the actor's face. This involves plastering on layers of
terracotta-coloured goo, rather like the material dentists use for
taking impressions of teeth. If it is necessary to take a cast of the
whole face, then the poor actor has to sit there breathing through
tubes and keeping very still for about twenty minutes until the goo
has set. It is then used to make a plaster cast, and it is on this cast that
the effects are made, usually in latex. This is called prosthetic work.

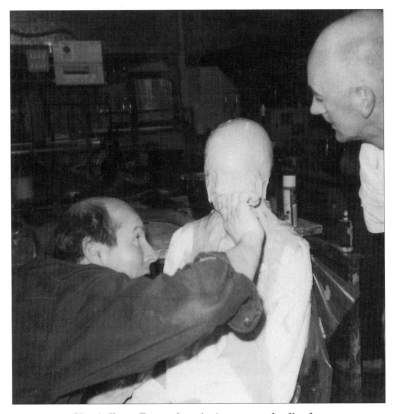

Visual effects – Frances Amey having a cast made of her face
for her rôle in *The Demon Headmaster*

In over twenty years of directing, I can remember it happening to only one of my actors. It was for the second series of *The Demon Headmaster*. This story described the villainous ex-headmaster taking over a genetic engineering company and creating a mutant cross between a lizard and Dinah, played by Frances Amey. In the final episode, this mutant, also played by Frances, had to age rapidly and crumble to dust whilst Dinah looked on in horror. In order to do this, we had to take a mould of Frances's face and make a brittle clay model, which was attached to part of an inflated weather balloon. When the air was sucked out of the balloon, the 'face' collapsed. Although taking the mould was an uncomfortable experience, Frances came through it smiling like a true 'pro'.

The whole effect meant that there was a lot of co-operation

between the Costume Designer, who had to provide a duplicate costume, the Make-up Designer, who had been making Frances's hair look thin, grey and aged, and the Visual Effects Designer, who had to make the effect work. There was then yet more work needed from the Video Effects Designer, to put the pictures together seamlessly so that Frances could appear to be in two places at once, and to allow the transition from Frances to the model also to be seamless. It took a long time to get things right. Tricks and effects usually do – they call for a great deal of patience from everyone.

Tutors and chaperones

It is likely that sometime before the rehearsal period starts, the tutor will get in touch. On any long-running project, the tutor should contact schools to ensure minimum disruption.

For some children, staying away from home in hotels, without their parents, may be a new experience. It is quite likely that chaperones will also try to speak to the parents or guardians of the children for whom they are to be responsible. Chaperones must be licensed and are employees of the Production, but they are paid to look after the interests of the children.

It is recognised that both parents of a child are not likely to be available to attend costume fittings, rehearsals and locations. It is usually the Production's responsibility to ensure that children are accompanied or transported safely.

The production team

As I've mentioned, there will be someone whose job it is to look after the actors. Regardless of job title, someone will be available to keep each actor in touch with the latest transport arrangements, call times and last-minute changes to the schedule. This person's first job is likely to be to call with details of the read-through or first rehearsal. He or she will be the principal point of contact for any queries or problems that crop up on long-running projects. Of course, in an emergency, many members of the team will do their best to help.

Prior commitments of the cast are always considered when a schedule is prepared. Sometimes an actor may be working for a few days on another project; sometimes people have holidays booked;

sometimes children have public exams to take. Wherever possible, the production has to work round these. If it is impossible, then it may be necessary to recast a particular actor. Usually, if we have enough notice, things can be made to work. I have been aware, though, of family holidays being altered, and I have known of families going away without the child I needed for my project. I don't think this has ever caused problems – it is a matter of priorities.

That is about all. Apart from a request for a medical certificate that may mean a visit to the GP, things should be ready for the first rehearsal.

10 *Rehearsals*

The read-through

Many drama-style productions will have a read-through.* This may be the only time the entire cast meets. The purpose is to read the script or set of scripts from beginning to end. It is not a performance and it is not truly a rehearsal, so there is nothing necessarily definitive in any of the readings. There is enough for the director to hear for the first time just what the script sounds like in the mouths of the cast, and for the cast to hear how their parts fit into the whole.

The scripts will be timed. The writers are usually invited to hear how the script works and to consider any problems. There is no action in a read-through, so the script will take less time to read than it will to perform. Even so, an experienced director will be able to tell if there is too much script or too little. The writer then has the chance to suggest cuts or to add extra material.

Other people present should be the whole production team, Costume and Make-up Designers, possibly the set designer and tutors and chaperones. This is the time to put faces to the names on letters and to the voices on the telephone.

Quite often this is all the rehearsal there is before shooting begins. There are very few dramas, films or stories that I can think of where characters are not known to each other, but it often happens that actors turn up on the set to be introduced to their husbands, wives, sons, fathers, mothers or daughters. They then have to go straight into a scene of very close relationship with a total stranger! At least if you have met at a read-through, the ice will have been broken.

Before leaving a read-through, always check what the arrangements are about the call for when you are next needed.

---

* Sometimes the turn-round on long-running series may mean that most of the cast are off shooting other episodes, in which case the rest of the cast and the director will have to make do without a full read-through or without any at all.

Rehearsals

There will (almost) always be rehearsal in front of the camera or cameras before any particular sequence is recorded, whether that is in a television studio, on location or on a film stage. But this section is about rehearsals before filming or recording days. It is sometimes called 'outside rehearsal' because it is away from (or outside) any studio.

Rehearsal rooms

To rehearse, you need space. If Production can arrange it, this space will be

* warm
* clean
* have access to telephones
* have tea and coffee facilities
* be close to a reasonably priced lunch and
* it will also be close to good public transport.

What can you expect to find in an average rehearsal room? Not a lot, is the answer. It is likely that as you walk in, the room will appear to be cluttered by chairs, tables, boxes and poles scattered round the room seemingly at random, and there may well be lines of coloured tape on the floor.

The lines represent the walls of the different sets – one colour for each set. Where there is enough space, everything is marked up to its full ground area and everything is in its right place. So, if there is an entrance hall, a living room and a kitchen with doors between, it should be possible to walk from one to another just as if the walls were really there. The poles are there to show doorways, pillars or perhaps the boundary of the set. The furniture is placed to give a good idea of where the designer will put the real furniture.

Ideally, there will be a room set aside for tuition. Sometimes this can be done entirely in the morning, allowing the director to rehearse in the afternoon, or the other way round. Sometimes, the rehearsals go on all day with children being released to the tutor for half-hour periods at a time. This only works where the story calls for two or more groups of children to work separately. *Grange Hill* is a good example. Directors can work with the 'Year 8's for a while then release them to tuition and then work on the story involving the 'Year 9's.

Sometimes a director will make the rehearsals very informal. Andrew told me about the first part he got. 'They didn't call it a rehearsal, but every Saturday for a three-week period, we'd get to know the characters – my "sister" and her "boyfriend". And I'd get to know the director, and we'd practise the scenes – the scenes out of the script.'

Rehearsing

I started in television production by working in BBC multi-camera studios in London and in the outside rehearsal rooms there. It was later that I moved on to work on location. Usually, there is more time given to rehearsal for multi-camera work than for single camera. Often, there is no outside rehearsal time at all for single-camera shoots. I believe it is a good idea to have even a few days of rehearsal before embarking on a shoot lasting for several weeks. In the end, I think it saves time on location and gives a better result – especially with children. Why?

Outside rehearsal is a time when director and actors can get to know one another, can explore the characters and the text. It is a time when they can start to work out how to play a scene, where they want to move, how they need to handle props. It is a time when problems can show up and be solved: suppose a character enters a house and has to remove a coat whilst talking to a second character who is in the kitchen. Suppose there is a line like, 'There you are. Can you pass the dish from the top shelf?' It may be that there is not time to take off and hang up a coat before that line is due. It may take time to get the timing right and natural-looking.

I sometimes begin rehearsals with children who are supposed to be related by playing games based on improvisation. It helps everyone to relax.

Next, I start the rehearsal proper. This means going through each scene, with everyone holding a script – no-one is expected to know the lines yet. As we go through, we look at the stage directions and work out moves. Often, the way each actor says the lines will be fine. Often, too, something will strike me, and I'll ask for a particular meaning to come out, or for a particular word to be stressed.

If the rehearsals are brief, before a long shoot, there will not be enough time to rehearse everything. Some scenes may be too short or too straightforward to merit the time. Some scenes may be too

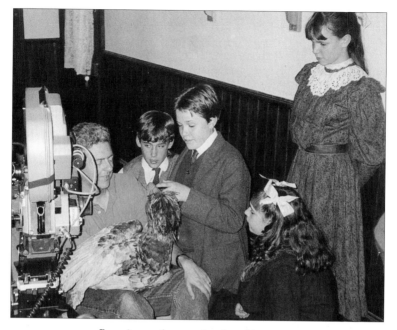

Preparing to rehearse on location with puppets.
Child actors in *The Phoenix and the Carpet*

complicated physically to rehearse – those with a lot of movement, or a lot of action that would have to be changed on location anyway. It may not be possible to have all the members of the cast for all scenes. So we select scenes to fit those who are available. I try and make sure we work through the moves (that is, we 'block' the moves) for sequences that may be emotionally complicated or that show up relationships. On *The Demon Headmaster*, we spent some time on the hypnosis sequences, both for Terrence Hardiman as the one hypnotising and for Frances Amey as the one being hypnotised. We also tried to work out a way for the actors whose characters had been hypnotised to behave.

There will be a list of scenes to rehearse each day. Whether this is in the director's head alone or typed out so everyone is in on the secret will vary from production to production. I would try and rehearse in story order from the beginning of the first episode through to the end of the last episode over the whole period. Sometimes, it may make sense to change this so we do not call an actor at 09.30 for one scene, and then keep him or her hanging around until 17.00 to rehearse the next scene with the same character. Sometimes, hanging around is unavoidable.

I enjoy rehearsals. There is not the pressure of recording. It is a time to work with just the actors and the script, without worrying about the technicalities. I do that back at the office. Part of my job is working out how to move the cameras to cover each scene so that the audience sees what it wants to see: where we are; this person saying a line; that person's reaction; this piece of paper that a character has just found; that alien coming through the window ... and so on.

The script

It is wise to make notes in the script of what happens at rehearsal – to underline words that need to be emphasised, to note starting positions and moves as well as changes to the dialogue. A good writer's scripts will not need much changing, but odd phrases may prove difficult. Sometimes it may be the actor who has a problem with a particular line; sometimes it is in the writing. One writer I knew was from Liverpool, writing for London children. Some of his phrases seemed to fit a Liverpudlian speech rhythm, but not a London rhythm. We had to make several changes. In a period adaptation, a word may simply have fallen out of fashion. Sometimes it helps to explain such a word or phrase; sometimes it is better to cut the problem out.

After the read-through, the scriptwriter may have alterations to make. All being well, these should come through before rehearsal is finished, so that the cast can go away with the script in its most up-to-date form.

Long and short rehearsals

By the end of a short rehearsal, the actors will already be able to get through some of their scenes without their scripts. On a location single-camera shoot, the main time for learning seems to be the night before the scenes are shot (or over breakfast). So far, we have not been forced into having to record more material than children can learn in an evening. It doesn't seem to cause major problems but it does take self-discipline and organisation. Those who, through laziness, do not learn their lines will not be popular with the rest of the cast and crew!

Some dramas are still recorded with several cameras. Ideally, this means each scene can be recorded in one go. This method is good if there are not too many sets or too much action. We can record fifteen or twenty minutes a day by this method, but you would be doing well to average more than five minutes or so on single camera, given the restriction on children's hours that we have in the UK. If there are many effects and crowd scenes, the average could be even lower.

Rehearsing for a multi-camera set-up

Clearly, all the actors need to know more script for a multi-camera recording. If the director is going to make everything work and use three or four cameras on most of the scenes without the cameras seeing each other, then there has to be a lot of careful planning. The plans only work if all the actors know exactly what they are going to do. This takes much more rehearsal than I would use before a single-camera shoot.

By the end of the rehearsal period, all the actors will know their script; they will know their moves; they will be able to give a consistent performance as often as necessary. A lot of drama is about people's reactions to what is going on – there may even be a comment in the script. If there has been a good reaction to something in rehearsal, the director may ask to see it again in the recording – and it will be necessary to have that reaction at the same moment each time the script is rehearsed or recorded. This is because a vision mixer will have a script that says there will be a reaction at 'this' moment. At 'this' moment, the Vision Mixer will cut to the camera that is showing the reaction. If the reaction is early or late, we will not see it.

I realise this may all sound daunting. It is up to the director, though, to make clear exactly what he or she wants, and to guide actors through. Of course, at rehearsal, the director will listen to what the actor has to say. It is not a matter of the director dictating how everything should be done. It is a multi-way creative process and I want all actors, adults and children, to feel that what they are doing is good.

Mostly I'd say, 'If one thing does not work, try another way.'

Often, the way this flexibility shows on a long-running series is that characters develop and grow closer to those of the actor, who bends his or her performance towards the character as written by the writers. The writers are usually happy to make the character work to the strengths of the actor.

RUNS AND RUN-THROUGHS

With the short rehearsal that may come before location work, I try to make sure that we read through all the scripts once more before the start of shooting. This helps fix the overall story in everyone's mind, and gives space for questions and discussion about problems. It only works if there are enough people around to be able to read most of the scenes. Here, I would not expect to have a run-through.

In contrast, at the end of rehearsals before going into a multi-camera recording, I would expect to 'run through' all the scenes to be recorded with only the shortest pauses for the resetting of props and furniture. I am used to doing two versions of these runs; one is the Technical Run and the other is the Producer's Run.

Technical Run

Up to this point, only the cast, the director and the chaperones will have been present with the AFM (if it is a BBC production) or the Stage Manager (if it is an ITV production). The Production Assistant and the Production Manager (or First) might drop in. At the Technical Run, a whole gang of people will arrive. These include set, costume, make-up and lighting designers, sound supervisor, senior cameraman, property buyer and floor assistant (or AFM – in ITV). In addition, the rest of my production team should be there: production manager (or floor manager), Production Assistant and any other interested parties.

Sometimes, these run-throughs are a little confusing for the actors because – probably for the first time – we work through in the RECORDING ORDER. This is exactly what it says it is. The recording order is worked out so that all the scenes with children may be completed by the time they should finish; it is also the order that reduces costume, make-up and set changes to the minimum. So, if there is a sequence of scenes in the story that starts off with children waking up in bed, then shows the characters dressed and ready for school, then shows them at the end of the day about to go to bed again, we would probably do both bedroom scenes together. This would save the time of one costume change. Over a whole studio day, these timesavings make a big difference.

It can get to be quite a headache, working out the best order.

Producer's Run

At another time, I would expect to organise a Producer's Run. Directors are responsible for working with the actors and technicians to turn the script into a film, programme or advert. The director may work on an entire series or only on a part. A Producer is responsible for putting a deal together. The Producer is legally and financially responsible for the production, but does not work with the actors or make the day-to-day 'artistic' or 'craft' decisions. On a long-running project, the Producer may have to look after a bigger group of episodes than the director. An Executive Producer is responsible for a whole series or may even have two or three series – or more – to consider. Both Producer and Executive Producer are interested in quality control, making sure the director is making a good show. The Producer and Executive Producer are also concerned on a long-running series that the director (who is familiar with only his or her part in the project) does not ask the actors to do anything inconsistent with what their characters have done in other episodes.

Either or both of these people may be present at a Producer's Run, and they will almost certainly want to see the script performed in story order.

Sometimes, the jobs of director and producer overlap. In this case, the project may be run by a Producer/Director. That is how I have often worked, with the Executive Producer being responsible for several projects, and just turning up for the Producer's Run.

After both types of Run, it is usual for the cast to be given a break so the director can talk over the results with either the technical crew or the Producer. In either case, there may be notes for the director (especially from the Producer). The cast would then come back for notes from the director that incorporate anything that may be necessary from the Producer.

Ideally, there would be time to re-rehearse any scenes where the producer wanted a significant change. Often, in practice, in a show centred on children I would only have time to give a verbal note. I would postpone altering a moment of performance, then, to the studio day.

Incidentally, anything that a director says to an actor about the way to say a line, the timing of a move, the pacing of a performance or the handling of a prop would be a 'note'. The actor may rely on memory for this or may make a pencilled note in the script. Pencil is probably better than pen because it is easier to rub out when, umm, IF the director changes his or her mind.

VARIATIONS

Different companies have different methods but most of the steps I have described should be there in some form or other.

One particular variation that may become more popular is the 'standing set'. It is possible to hire a simple film stage*, build the set there and keep it there. It is also possible to bring in the two or three cameras, as you need them. This makes it economical for some pro-grammes to rehearse for a few days on the actual set they will use, without lights, costumes or make-up, then to bring in the camera equipment and crew and to record a couple of episodes over two days. The BBC-Disney co-production called *Microsoap* was made like this.

In most multi-camera studios, the sets are brought in and set up just for the recording days, then taken out so that the studio can be used for other programmes until the next time. The BBC series *The Wild House* and Carlton's *Welcome to orty-Fou* were made like this.

A very short project requiring only a day or two on a film stage may not need a read-through or an outside rehearsal.

You may hear about other variations and different ways of mixing the ingredients. If there is time to rehearse, we should be grateful. It is, truly, quality time with the script.

But what about the shoot, the recording, the location and the studio? That is another chapter.

---

* There is more about film studios and stages in chapter 12.

11 *This is it!*

Things move fast in television. The hardware available to us changes every year – and the software more often than that. Going onto the set and acting in front of the camera changes in lots of ways over the years, but it always boils down to three things – people, acting and cameras. There are a lot of variations on how people get different results so some readers of this book may find their experiences do not quite tally with every aspect of the experiences related here. There should be enough, though, to give you an impression of what it is like working with cameras.

There are two main ways of shooting drama – and lots of variations.

The method that has been around the longest – about a hundred years – is *single-camera.*

The other method is *multi-camera.*

Single-camera shooting is extremely flexible and can be done just about anywhere on earth. This method is used in film studios, too. (More accurately, I should write 'sound stages'. It would be correct to say, 'Such-and-such film studios have ten sound stages.')

Multi-camera shooting is most often done in television studios. BBC Television Centre for instance, had eight main television studios last time I looked, as well as news studios and presentation areas. It is also possible to use multi-camera techniques on location. Even then, I think most people find work on location feels very different from any kind of studio work.

Multi-camera recording

Multi-camera television studios contain an awful lot of expensive equipment and they need a lot of people to run them. They are therefore expensive to hire, and a Production will want to have as few days in them as possible and to record as much material as possible in the time they do have.

A number of tv companies as well as the BBC have buildings called Television Centres. Though these vary in size, all Television Centres have a lot in common. I will take the BBC's version as my main reference.

The day begins

If you are working in a multi-camera drama set-up, the actors are almost certainly going to rehearse well away from the studio. On the last day of rehearsal, someone on the production will give all the actors their call times to be at the studio. There will also be information about transport, if a car is to be hired, or about car parking, if the chaperone is to bring any of the children.

So, on the day, you turn up at the Main Reception and check in with Security. Once you're let into the building, you go to the Stage Door to collect your dressing-room key.

Since a chaperone can look after up to twelve named children, it is quite common for children to share dressing rooms, boys with boys and girls with girls. Tutors are limited in the numbers they can teach; they need rooms to teach in and these are often dressing rooms. This means a production with a lot of child actors will need more dressing rooms than similar productions without children. Most dressing rooms should have somewhere to hang 'day clothes', enough chairs for everyone in the room and a washhand basin or two. Most will have a large mirror with good lighting. There should also be a card on the door with the names of the actor or actors who should be in that room.

There should be somewhere open for refreshments and there will be showers and lavatories not far from the dressing room. If the journey in has been long and difficult, many people like to grab a drink before they start dressing and make-up. The call time is usually the time to turn up in the make-up room or in the costume room.

The costumes to be worn that day may also be in the dressing room, correctly labelled. Quite often, though, children will be taken to Wardrobe (this is the costume room close to the studio where the Costume Designer and the dr   ers are based). It should be quite clear whether any particular child is expected to change in the dressing room or in the Wardrobe. There should be somebody looking after actors who is around in the studio or in the dressing-room area to answer queries. Most often, actors have to put on most of the costume except perhaps for jackets or other 'top layer', before going in to make-up. On a production of any size, there will be a Make-up Designer and one or more assistants. Usually, the Designer and the assistant have agreed which actors they will look after and they will stick to this for the whole production. All the make-up artists I have met have been pleasant people, very easy to get on with, who enjoy their work. Part of their job is to help actors relax as they get into character.

For a modern piece, very little make-up should be needed. Most attention will probably go on the hair, to make sure that it stays consistent from scene to scene throughout the production. Sometimes a little base make-up is needed on boys to reduce any tendency to shine or to compensate for looking too pale under the bright lights. Fair eyebrows may need darkening but, on the whole the most natural effects can be achieved by applying the least amount of make-up possible. Sometimes, the Make-up Designer will ask to see actors before the studio day to give (or to supervise) a haircut.

A 'straight' make-up will take only a few minutes. If there are period make-ups to apply, or special effects, like wounds, they will take longer. One boy I had working on a play in Bristol needed make-up applied to his chest to look as though he had just had open-heart surgery. He also needed to look a little blue at times, because of the heart condition. Similarly, Frances Amey in *The Demon Headmaster* second series had to play both Dinah and Eve, the genetic mutant lizard-girl. Not only was Eve part-lizard, she also had to age prematurely. Frances had to have latex scales and a progressively older 'look' applied to her face. There was also the matter of her scaly hand.* To make her hair look thinner and grey, she also had a latex bald cap over her hair plus a thin grey wig. This all took a long time. As it happened, this was a series shot on single camera, but complex make-ups (like the operation scar) are also possible for television studio work. (There is more about Frances's make-up on p. 102.)

Some time ago, I directed a series called *Watt on Earth*. This featured an ordinary family and an alien who called himself Watt. Although he appeared to be human, this was not his natural form. Because in his own terms he was very young, he could never quite get his appearance right, whatever shape he appeared in. As a human, in the first series, his ears were back to front. In the second series, he

---

* Compared with the face mould, this was easy – it was just a matter of taking a cast of Frances's hand and making a scaly 'glove'.

was doing better, and they were the right way round, but green. The actor who played Watt, Garth Napier Jones, always had to turn up early to have his ears done. He is an adult actor, so we did not run into problems with the number of hours in his day as we would have done with a child.

When make-up is complete, it is time to finish off the costume. If there is anything unusual or complicated, like a period costume, the dressers will help or advise. It is their job both to look after the costumes and to help actors get them right.

Rehearsals

Because everything should always be beautifully planned for television, the people needed in the first sequence to be recorded should be the ones ready by the scheduled start time. Those in later sequences may still be in Wardrobe or Make-up. In theory, as soon as the actors are ready, they should return to their dressing rooms to wait to be called by the Floor Assistant or Runner.

Often, there is some sort of Green Room or waiting area close to the studio and that may be a better place to wait. As children have a chaperone, it will be her decision and, of course, they may have tuition, more of which later.

Next comes the call into the studio. Studios used for drama tend to be big. The acting area of the largest studio at the BBC's Television Centre is around twenty-seven metres by twenty-seven. When they are empty, the drama studios all feel huge. When they have a set in them, they feel cluttered. You open the door into the studio, and, as often as not, there just in front of your nose is a 'cyc' or cyclorama – it is a large plain backcloth, usually lit to look like sky.

The next thing to strike people new to the studio is the large area of plain, unpainted wooden flattage. This is the back of the scenery, much of which is made from large sheets of flat plywood fastened to timber frames. The other side, which the cameras see, will be painted or papered to look like a solid room.

The floor under your feet is heavy-duty lino, often grey. It has to be smooth for the cameras to move easily over it. Within the sets, though, it will be painted perhaps to look like tiles or wood. Sometimes, the set designer arranges to have large sheets of vinyl or sticky-backed plastic on the floor instead of paint. These are a little more expensive and can tear, causing problems, but it does have an advantage over floor paint. If you spill anything on floor paint, the paint dissolves and becomes a sticky, slippery mess. This and the fact that tv studios have a great deal of electrical equipment in them explains why it is forbidden to take any drinks into the studio.

The Floor Assistant will guide the actors to the right starting place on the set. Newcomers will be aware that the set seems to be different from what they were expecting. They will also notice the bright lights (slung from the grid that is suspended below the roof), the cameras, the microphone booms and the people, some of whom will be scurrying around finishing off the fine detail on the set. Some will be putting on headsets by their cameras. Some will be standing around waiting for their turn to scurry.

Somewhere you will see whoever is going to be the floor manager. This is the person responsible for everything happening on the floor – for safety, for keeping things moving and for relaying the director's wishes to anyone not on a headset. I normally expect my Production Manager or First Assistant to be my Floor Manager, but there are people who do nothing but work in the studio who may also have that title and do that job.

Equipment

The cameras these days are not particularly big, but in the average studio they have various bits bolted on to them that you would not see on the same camera used on location. These include big viewfinders and long handles with controls for zooming and focusing the lens. Often, the cameras will be mounted on heavy pedestals that glide smoothly across the floor, and allow the camera to elevate and depress (go up and down).

Sound is picked up by microphones. These microphones are often hung from booms, long arms supported by wheeled platforms. The operator stands on the platform and can turn and tilt the mike and extend or retract the boom arm to follow the action almost anywhere on the set. If there is not much room, it may be easier to use 'fishing rods', extendable poles with a microphone at the end that one of the sound assistants will hold out of shot but close enough to the actors.

If there are major problems with a complicated move, it may be necessary to use radio mikes. These are a nuisance because they have to be concealed within the actor's costume, and the batteries need changing fairly often. They are useful in the right place, though.

Directing in the studio

Some directors like to start their rehearsals directing from the floor. I do, at least for the first scene. This way, the actors can see one familiar face as they start their day!

On the first day of a new production, everything is unfamiliar. The camera crew will gradually get to know the cast and to know the best positions to place their cameras to get the best shots. There will be a lot of stopping and starting as positions of furniture and props are adjusted so that everything works as it did at rehearsal.

Once we are into the swing of things, I stay in the control gallery. What I usually want first is for the actors to walk through the first scene, saying their lines and moving more deliberately or slowly than they should. Often when there is a move, there will be a cry of 'Hold it!' from the Floor Manager, and everything stops whilst I try to explain what I wanted. Because we use three or four cameras most of the time, we have a control gallery where the Vision Mixer sits. He or she has to switch from one camera to the next as the scene moves forward so that the audience can see what they need to in order to understand the story. Sometimes it needs the actors to do a move two or three times to get the cameras, the Vision Mixer and the sound team synchronised.

Once all the initial problems have been ironed out, we run the scene from beginning to end. After that it should just be a case of giving final notes, resetting the props, checking costume and make-up, and we are ready for recording. The final note may be something like, 'When you open the drawer, make sure you remember to stand to the left so we can see past you into it.' It may be something to do with performance, like, 'Remind ... that I really want to see how upset she is. She's just got home from school where she lost her English project when the school computer crashed.' Or, it may be a general note to the whole cast, to, '... keep the pace up'. This just means, 'Don't slow down.'

Recording

And so the big moment arrives. We begin the recording. In the UK, it is normal to record onto tape in multi-camera studios. The floor manager will shout, 'Stand by, studio. We're going for recording. Quiet please ... I said, QUIET. Stop that banging. Sorry, Roger. Will you stop that hammering NOW. We are about to record. Thank you, that's better.'

This is perfectly normal. It does not help to calm the nerves, but phrases like this, not necessarily in this order, are familiar from almost every recording I have directed. Sometimes, of course the hammering is in another part of the building and may take a while to find, so we can stop it. The actors have to ignore it and concentrate on creating the right mood for the story.

Whilst all this is going on, the technical manager in the gallery has run the recording machine (or machines). The floor manager will then say something like, 'We're at speed [referring to the recording machines]. This is scene 305, shots 1 to 15, take 1. Stand by.'

Everything has gone very quiet.

In the gallery, the director says, 'Cue them!'

The floor manager says nothing more, but makes a sweeping gesture with her hand and arm – a clear, unmistakable sign. The scene begins.

I try to arrange things so that actors do not have to begin straight after a cue simply with a word. Instead, I try and find something for them to do. So 'father' can be in the kitchen and, on cue, will pour hot

Studio drama – a moment from
Carlton Television's *Welcome to orty-Fou*

water into his mug. At the same time, his 'daughter' will enter from the hallway and start speaking. I can cut out some of the action in the edit, but at least the scene should look as though it has started naturally, not as though someone has said, 'Start acting.'

At the end of the scene or sequence, the floor manager says, 'Hold it there, thank you. How was that, Roger?'

If all has gone well, we move on. If something has gone wrong, we can do the whole scene again. Sometimes, this is the easiest thing for the actors. Sometimes, we pick it up in the middle. If this is the case, I look for a point just before things go wrong but that will make sense to the actors. The floor manager would say, 'OK, we're going from shot 10. Take it from 'father's' line, "So what did Melanie say?" We're just running to record. OK, here we go … This is a pick-up from shot 10. Stand by.'

Once again, there will be a silent cue and the scene continues. Because it takes the actors a moment or two to get up to speed, as it were, we always overlap the action, knowing that the first moments of the retake won't be used.

If all is well, we stop the tape and check it, making sure that the recording is 'clean'. Then the floor manager will call, 'That's clear, everybody. On to scene 8, shot 16. John and Jill to tuition, please.'

And so it goes on, all day, scene by scene until the whole programme is recorded.

This system is known as 'rehearse-record', because that is exactly what you do. Once each scene is recorded, it is finished, at least so far as the actors are concerned.

To keep things moving, it is good to use three or four cameras. There are times, though, when we shoot odd shots just on one camera. This often happens in a confined space like a hall or stairway. It may also be easier or safer to use just one camera to cover effects shots that need treatment later, or shots where the action is messy and difficult to do again. Sometimes, in these circumstances, we use two (or more) cameras to record two (or more) different angles or versions of the action, and cut them together later.

There are all kinds of variation possible and to go into them all would be confusing – even for me. It should be possible in rehearsal to explain not only what we want but also how we are going to achieve it. It often helps to explain all the hows and whys as we go along. Sometimes, that is confusing, and I find myself saying something like, 'Trust me. Do it this way, and it will look great – we'll add the explosion later.'

After the last scene has been recorded, everything – including the scenery – will be packed away *fairly* carefully until the next time. Several series I have directed worked on a two-week turn-round. We would rehearse thoroughly one week and the second would be given to the run-throughs and a two- or three-day studio recording session. The next Monday we went back to the rehearsal rooms and began again. Certainly at the BBC's Television Centre, it used to be normal for there to be a whole string of shows in the studio we had been using, from *Blue Peter* to a situation comedy or two.

Variations

Effects

It is quite normal to have sequences shot on location and added to those shot in the studio. The more there is on location, the less material needs to be recorded in the studio. This makes either for shorter studio days or for more complicated set-ups. *On Watt on Earth*, we had a lot of effects, which were mostly to do with Watt 'detransanimateobjectifying'. With a word like that, you might expect us to use a lot of time in the studio getting it right!

On the BBC adaptations of Allan Ahlberg's *Happy Families*, we had to shoot each story entirely in the studio. This included theatre interiors for *Mr and Mrs Hay the Horse*, a storm at sea for *Master Salt the Sailor's Son*, flying and car trips for *Master Money the Millionaire*, a cross-country run for *Mr Tick the Teacher* and an entire horse race for *Miss Jump the Jockey*. Most of the awkward scenes involved a technique called variously 'Blue-screen', 'Chroma-key' and 'CSO' (short for ' Colour Separation Overlay'). I'll stick to 'Blue-screen', as, currently, that seems to be the most widely used expression in television in the UK.

The Blue-screen process allows us to change a background to anything we like or anything we can imagine. The camera points at a large coloured screen, which is usually a particular shade of blue. It sees normally any people or objects placed in front of the screen (provided they – or clothes – are not that particular shade of blue!) There is a clever box of tricks that cuts out all the blue and allows us to 'paint in' any other background from any other source. On *Happy Families*, I used models. Many of these were drawings that had been cut out and glued to stiff board. To make streets, we had cut-out shops, houses and objects such as a postbox. These could all be arranged in different layouts for different scenes. We also had a large picture of sky to go behind everything else.

It was possible to build up layers of picture electronically. For a car ride, we had trees and telegraph poles whizzing past in the foreground. These were more card cut-outs on a blue background. Behind this layer we had the car. This was a cut-out about twelve centimetres long and five centimetres high. The next layer showed the actors against blue, sitting on blue blocks. The car hid most of their bodies, so we could see just heads and shoulders, as if they were in a real car. Behind that came the countryside. This was a long strip of thin card, painted and glued to a large drum that rotated horizontally. With the foreground and the background both moving, it did look as though our camera was travelling fast alongside the car.

This is complicated. More elaborate effects shots like this are used in many films. There is a shot in *The Titanic* where the camera appears to start low in front of the ship and to swoop up and round behind the ship allowing it to pass through the frame, with people walking on deck. Only the two people right on the prow of the ship were real, and the only solid bit of ship for that shot was the prow. The camera did swoop round up and behind the actors, but everything else in this shot, including the crew and other passengers used a sophisticated version of the Blue-screen technique and very clever computer graphics.

What has this got to do with actors? Most of the actors I know find it harder to work with Blue-screen than in normal sets. The children in *The Phoenix and the Carpet* had to fly on their carpet to many places and to look with interest at what they were flying past, over or through. In reality, the actors were on the carpet, but their only background was blue. They had to imagine everything else. The only way for the actors to see themselves as the audience would see them was on a tv screen. They couldn't look at this *and* act. In any case, the final picture was probably not available until the programme had been edited.

The possibilities for Blue-screen seem to be endless. In the early days, we couldn't move the cameras on the foreground very much, because it wasn't usually possible to make background movement match. Now, there are all sorts of camera rigs or mounts that give us a huge amount of flexibility. It is even possible to work in a 'virtual studio', where people can move around in a totally blue set and where we can cut from one camera to another whilst the computer-generated background changes to match the action. It is even possible to make the actors disappear behind virtual pillars.

To make all this convincing, the actors have to move and speak perfectly naturally, whilst imagining where they are in relation to the non-existent set. It is no use saying, 'OK, see you.' And heading for the 'door', if the door – which the actor cannot see – is on the other side of the picture!

The way the director helps the actor is to explain, perhaps with sketches or a model, what is going to APPEAR to happen. In addition, the Floor Manager will make sure that there are marks on the floor (that will not show on camera) where there should be doors, windows, pillars and furniture.

Blue-screen allows all kinds of things to happen that would be impossible in real life, or that would otherwise be too expensive to stage. Some child actors never come across it. Some may feel they can never escape it. The essence of it for the actor, I think, is to have in mind a clear image of the setting and to let the imagination do the work. The director should be able to help, and there will probably be a chance to see the set without actors on a tv monitor.

AUDIENCES

Some tv programmes work best if they have an audience. Games shows, 'people shows' and situation comedies probably head the list. All of these may include children, but it would normally only be the situation comedies that would need child actors. It is still possible to pre-record scenes in the way I described for 'rehearse-recordings'. Scenes with young children probably would be pre-recorded. Children under 13 have to be away from the studios by 5.00 p.m., so there is little choice. There is more about this in chapter 5.

The problem is that most sitcoms begin their recording between 7.00 and 8.00 p.m. A studio laid out for an audience will have all the sets lined up so the audience can see most of what is going on. They sit on raised seating that usually fills nearly half the studio. Over their heads are loudspeakers so they can hear what is going on, and tv monitors so they can see not only what is going on, but also see any scenes played in that were recorded earlier or on location. There are microphones over the audience, too, and these pick up the audience reaction, laughter and applause (if any).

Older children, between 13 and 16 years old, may be allowed to work as late as 10.00 p.m., and so may be able to take part in an evening recording. If this does happen, then the scenes are rehearsed during the day, in the recording order. If all goes well, there should be a 'dress run' late in the afternoon to make sure everything works. There will then be time for a quick meal and notes from the director.

Once recording starts, scenes should run together with few interruptions. Anyone who has watched *Auntie's Bloomers* or *It'll be all right on the Night* knows that things often do not run smoothly. If a mistake happens, whether it is an actor's mistake or one of the crew's, the thing is to keep concentration, listen for the point where the director wants to pick the scene up, and try and get it right the second time with as little fuss as possible. On the whole, if these errors are funny, they are so only to the people who were there.

Acting the show for the first time with an audience can be unnerving. If a line gets a big laugh, it may be hard to carry on without drawing breath and giving room for the laugh. The director should be aware of the problem in the rehearsal stage. Adult actors will probably have the experience to cope. Because they want the show to go well – as well as being generally good-natured, most will be helpful to less experienced actors. If there should be unwanted pauses, it may be possible to cut them out later. On the whole, it is better with an audience not to have to do a retake. It is also possible to add an audience reaction at the edit.

Other matters

No child is permitted to work for more than an hour at a time. Those under 13 should have rest breaks more frequently than that. Every child will be the responsibility of a chaperone, and the chaperone should prompt Production if she feels a child needs a break. On my own productions, where the writers are aware of the problems, it has usually been possible to break the script down in such a way that most scenes can be rehearsed and recorded in an hour or less. I find that breaking halfway through a scene or between the rehearsal and the recording of a scene wastes a lot of time.

On the other hand, I have hardly ever asked a child to wait for a lavatory break. It does not seem reasonable to expect a child to give a good performance whilst uncomfortable.

The chaperone has parental duties and, although employed by Production, must be listened to. The children, too, MUST listen to the chaperone and do as they are told. That is part of the deal. Television studios have a lot of high voltage equipment and there are cables running all over the place. It is a legal requirement that there are proper fire lanes and emergency exits, and these must be kept clear of obstruction. In the studio, safety is the floor manager's responsibility, and the children are the chaperone's responsibility. I have seen one child, a regular 'extra', sent off the set 'never ever to return' for larking about and ignoring the chaperones as well as everybody else.

Unless schools under the tv studio's local education authority are on holiday, the Production Company has to provide classrooms and tutors sufficient to teach all the children on the show. This means that we have to find time to send each child away for lessons. These lessons should not be less than 30 minutes in length. There should be an average (over two weeks) of 3 hours' tuition a day. It is not always possible to squeeze six 30-minute periods into a studio day that has to finish no later than 5 p.m. (for under 13s). This does not matter provided tuition hours over each two-week period average 3 hours a day.

Local Authority inspectors are authorised to visit any studio or location. They may ask to see the record of each child's work. If they are not satisfied, they can stop any child from working on the show. On a children's drama, that could easily destroy the production. In this book, several people say education is important – at the very least to keep open the options for each child actor. It is a serious matter both for us and for the child actor.

Acting on camera

Some children seem to be able to act very well. Others, perhaps not so well. No producer or director is going to give a child a major rôle in any kind of production unless confident that the child chosen will be able to give the performance wanted. It does not matter, then, whether a child is a first-time professional or has been acting since he was 6. We would not choose you unless we thought you could act as we wanted!

Acting is something that can be refined and developed. There are things you can do to develop vocal range and skills like singing, dancing or even fencing. What I cannot do in this book is to teach anyone *how* to act. It is possible, though, to offer a few pointers about the difference between acting on stage and acting in front of the camera.

On stage, you need to speak up – ideally, to project your voice so that you can be heard at the back of the auditorium without a microphone. This technique can be learned. Often, though, children are given radio microphones so their voice can be boosted without projection. On stage, too, a tiny facial reaction is not going to be noticed. Instead of a raised eyebrow, you may have to move the whole head. It is possible to do this with great subtlety. It is up to the director to help make clear what is necessary.

On television, the camera may be less than a metre from the actor's eyes. The microphone is no further from his (or her) mouth. There is no need to project. There is no need to exaggerate reactions. The camera sees all. Even a tiny reaction such as widening the eyes slightly or the tiniest of frowns may be important. I think it is because I look for very subtle reactions that my choice of children from a drama class may surprise a school drama teacher. There is a difference between a good tv performance and a good stage performance.

The microphone hears all, usually. It may be necessary to speak up in noisy conditions, such as at a party with background music, or in a busy school corridor. The way television works, the director may ask for the actors to speak up AS THOUGH the music or that background chatter were there, and rather loud. It may be easier to add these effects later in the dubbing process, so it may feel rather odd. It is a decision for the director on advice from the sound recordist.

Sometimes, too, a director may ask for a move to be slowed down. Young people can move fast – too fast, sometimes, for the camera operators to keep up. Getting up out of a chair, therefore, is one of the things that may need to be slowed down slightly, so that it looks right on camera. This is an important point. Wherever the scene is shot, in the studio or on location, there is almost bound to come a point at which the director says, 'I know it feels natural to do that move in that way, but on camera, it looks better to do it this way.'

Marks

One of the points about multi-camera studios is that most scenes can be acted 'naturally', in real time. This is one of the contrasts with single-camera shooting, which I write about in the next chapter. One of the points that is common to both single- and multi-camera work is the business of 'marks'. It is so important that I think it deserves a section of its own.

The audience should not be aware of marks and actors should not seem to be aware of them either. There are three sorts of mark.

- Props and furniture may need to be marked. These things have to be moved in the action, and may end up with two or three marked positions. Sometimes a piece of scenery may have to be moved. This may need a mark, too.
- Camera positions may need marking. This is true on location if the camera is on a dolly (sturdy trolley), which needs to move. Cameras in multi-camera studios also may need marks, if their position is critical.
- People – actors – often need specific positions and these may need to be marked.

A multi-camera studio floor is usually made of lino, some of which may be painted. On a painted or unpainted lino floor the usual marker will be a wax crayon, a substance easily washed off when the production is finished.

Often, actors will be working on a floor covered by carpet or some other surface. For them, we often use a coloured tape, which can be removed without damaging the surface. Because it is important to get the position right with the actors standing in their normal positions, it is not the job of the actors to make their own marks. This will be done by the Floor Manager. On location, it can be helpful to have a solid object as the mark, which the actor may find with his foot.

Why do we bother? It is all a matter of making the pictures look right. I might have the camera looking over a girl's shoulder at a boy. If the boy and the girl stand still this is fine. But if the boy or the girl starts off by moving into position, there could be a problem. If the girl moves from out of shot into the right of frame and overshoots, she will obscure the boy. That means a retake. If she does not come far enough, then there will be an ugly space on the right of frame – and in any case, she could end up too far from the boy, perhaps, to take an apple from him when he hands it over.

Similarly, if the boy moves into shot from the left and overshoots, he will disappear behind the girl or be out of focus. If he does not come far enough, then the camera will see only half his face.

If there is a larger group, then it may be important that we see everybody clearly. The more heads there are, the more likely one is to obscure another.

It is important that the relationship between people, cameras and pieces of furniture is right to make the pictures work. Sometimes, an error of a couple of centimetres can spoil the shot. It is therefore important for actors to learn the importance of hitting their marks without appearing to look at them.

I have come across the odd child who did not seem to understand the importance of marks. There was one who treated missing his marks as a big joke. He wasted a lot of his time and everyone else's in rehearsing again and again until he got it right. I try and show the children I work with WHY it is important to hit marks. I make them stand in the position of the camera and look past me at one of their colleagues, while I show them what happens if I am or am not on my marks. It takes about two minutes. I think it is fair to say that all the children to whom I have demonstrated this have always tried to hit their marks and have understood my directions.

There are various tricks that help you to hit a mark without looking at the floor. One is to step onto the marks and then take two (or three) natural paces backwards. If you then take two (or three) natural paces forwards, you should hit the mark easily. Sometimes, it is only necessary to get the end of a movement into a position. It may then be possible to take half a pace out of the shot, leaving one foot in position. On 'Action', simply swing into position with the other foot.

Another trick is to use a piece of furniture as the mark. It may be that you need to end up by the corner of a table or behind a particular chair.

The point is that whatever you do at rehearsal will be needed again on the take – and it has to look fresh and spontaneous every time. For a studio production, the rehearsal period should make clear when many marks are likely to be necessary. The cameras are fairly mobile and will do what they can to compensate for errors, but the moves caused by compensating can look ugly. With single-camera shooting, marks are just as important – the camera is likely to be less fluid in its moves. A studio camera pedestal can often tweak a few centimetres in any direction. A carefully laid camera track is a different matter! It is almost more important to hit your marks on location. But there is more about single-camera work in the next chapter.

12 *This is it – on Location*

This chapter is about going on location with a single camera.* It is possible to shoot with two or even three cameras on location and this can speed up the process; from the actors' point of view, the big difference is probably less to do with the technology than to do with being on location.

The technology is changing fast. A lot of equipment is becoming cheaper and lighter and therefore more flexible. At the end of a shooting day, the result is still the same – we have recorded the performance of an actor or group of actors against some background or other. I think it is worth mentioning some of the different equipment and methods just for information and explaining the differences, for those who do not know, between film and tape.

Equipment and things

Film and its particular requirements

Film has been around longer than any other method of recording pictures. In the camera, light falls on an area of a long piece of clear plastic, which is coated in special chemicals that include a certain amount of silver. There are really only four sizes or gauges of film in common use in the whole world of television: 35 mm is restricted to high-budget projects, commercials and anything where film must be used with electronic or animated effects. 16 mm and super 16 are cheaper and much more widely used in television. High-budget, epic movies for the cinema on really big screens may use 70 mm film.

There are three main points about film.

---

* On a tv studio production, we have sometimes used a single camera to shoot sequences both on location and on a film sound stage. It does happen that we refer to the whole single-camera shoot inaccurately as 'on location'.

- Firstly, it is expensive compared with videotape. This means that we have to be very careful about how much we use. It is expensive just to leave the camera running, and the cost of the film in shooting a retake is significant. Working on film, I would perhaps rehearse more before 'Take 1' than I would with tape.
- Secondly, all television stations can broadcast film of either 16 mm or 35 mm gauge without any problem. Videotape comes in all sorts of formats and may have to be 'converted' before it is shown by a particular tv station. This means that a programme on film is slightly easier to sell abroad than one on videotape.
- And thirdly, there are many people who feel that film is just 'better' than videotape.

PHRASES TO DO WITH FILM

One thing that the technical crews have felt strongly about over the years is the word 'filming'. Really we should only use that word if we are actually using film, not videotape. If we use electronic cameras, then the correct expression should be 'recording'.

The standard reel holds about ten minutes' worth of film. This is including all the 'run-up', identification, stand-by and actual take time. Pauses to 'change rolls' are therefore quite frequent. There will usually be one or more assistant camera operators who have various jobs like focus pulling, looking after the clapper-board and changing rolls. Sometimes, you will see these people up to their elbows in a strange-looking black bag. This is when they are changing the film roll in the 'mag.' or magazine. This is the lightproof holder for the film that sits on top of or behind the main body of the camera.

Another job for the camera assistant is that of 'checking the gate'. The gate is the rectangular support that holds each frame of film steady and in place for the tiny moment (about a fiftieth of a second) that the action is exposed through the camera's lens and shutter. After each successful take, the camera operator will say, 'check the gate'. The assistant will take the lens off the camera and peer into the gap with a magnifying glass. Sometimes tiny flakes of the light-sensitive coating fall off the film and get stuck in the gate. If this happens at the beginning of a shot, we may be left with a black mark across part of the picture. Sometimes, the film may appear to be damaged by a scratch. If either of these things happen, the assistant will say either, 'Hair in the gate,' or 'There's a scratch.' The result for the actors is the same – another take.

Mounts

Both film and video cameras can be mounted on tripods, which are simply sets of legs that can be used at various heights. Sometimes, short legs are used. These are called 'baby-legs'. We can also put cameras on 'dollies', which are sturdy trolleys. These allow the camera to be pushed across a smooth surface or along a 'track' by the 'Grips' (the person responsible). Track is exactly what it sounds like – it looks like a narrow-gauge railway track. This can be laid on almost any surface and allows the camera to move very smoothly.*

Director Marilyn Fox prepares for a tracking shot in *Five Children and It*.

If the camera has to follow action through difficult areas, such as up and down steps, into or out of a house, we sometimes just ask the cameraman to carry the camera, in which case it is 'hand-held'. Sometimes, to make shots like this smoother, we use Steadicam. This is a heavy harness that the cameraman wears. From the harness there extends a spring-loaded arm on which the camera and a monitor can

---

* It is not usual in this country to see a film camera on a 'ped'. Peds are nearly always kept for video cameras in a multi-camera studio.

be mounted. The harness and the arm smooth out bumps and jolts caused as the camera operator is walking – or running.

Sometimes we use cranes. These come in all shapes and sizes. They can be used simply as a high platform. More often, they give great scope for moves to follow the performance, sometimes swooping into (or away from) the action. I like using cranes, but they do take a long time to set up.

Some cranes have seats behind the camera for the operator, a focus-puller and the director. Other forms of crane have a 'hot-head'. This is a remote-control device that allows the camera operator to stay on the ground and turn the camera any way that may be needed, to focus, zoom, stop and start the camera and so on. The hot-head is obviously much lighter than a seat and operator. The arm can therefore be longer or lighter (or both) and is able to move much more swiftly. There are a number of motorised computer-controlled rigs available now. You see them used in fast spectacular moves.

There are also special mounts that can be fixed to motor vehicles to show action inside them. There are mounts and cameras for almost any purpose you can imagine, from roundabouts to helicopters. We can even hire a special model helicopter not much more than a metre in length, and put a camera inside it to give affordable aerial shots.

You may hear, too, of a 'low-loader'. This is a low trailer on which we can put cars and small vans. There is enough room to put a camera almost anywhere around the vehicle, and for the crew. As the trailer is towed around the streets, the actors can act safely inside the vehicle without having to worry about actually driving.

You will hear the term 'film unit'. This means those working together on one project, on one site. When using video cameras, we use just the word 'unit'.

FILM STUDIOS

Another phrase you may come across is 'film stage'. Some tv studios were originally converted from film stages. The main difference is that film stages have little or no built-in equipment but they are sound proof – and are sometimes called 'sound stages'. There are film stages that aren't sound proofed and they're not used for dialogue. Some film stages are huge, much bigger than any purpose-built tv studio. When we talk about 'film studios', we often mean a group of film stages and various other facilities, usually including a large outdoor area (called 'the lot') that can have big exterior sets built on it.

Most film studios will also have a canteen or restaurant of some sort; most will have workshops; most will have some rooms for editing and dubbing.

There are a number of film studios, most of which are in the southeast of England. Pinewood, Elstree (not to be confused with BBC Elstree), Bray, Twickenham and Shepperton are all outside the London Underground network. There is a small complex at Wembley. In Ealing, West London, there are the Ealing Film Studios, which used to belong to the BBC. Both of these are within the Underground network.

Television centres tend to be relatively new, bright and shiny. Film studios tend to feel as though they need smartening up. The floors, in particular, are usually rough wooden planks, so we usually have to build a new false floor for each set.

Sometimes, a production may decide to hire an empty warehouse – or even an aircraft hangar – and use that as a 'sound stage'. It may be cheaper than hiring a properly built place but there can be problems. Because of the lack of soundproofing, shooting often has to stop if there is heavy rain. There will be too much noise from the roof to continue.

One of the more amusing aspects of making tv programmes, is that we often end up in improbable places.

'Going for a take' – on film

As in the studio, there is a very clear sequence of events between the rehearsal and a take. These days, quite a lot of crews trained on film cameras shoot happily with either film or tape. Sometimes, therefore, you may find there is little or no difference between a unit using a film camera and a unit using an electronic camera.

Once the director is happy with the actors' performances and the camera team is happy with the camera moves, the First Assistant tells everyone to stand by for a take. Costume and make-up staff rush in for last-minute checks and everyone sets up from the top, or beginning, of the shot. Once everyone is set, the director or the First Assistant calls, 'Turn over.' The cameraman starts the camera and the sound recordist starts the sound recorder. When their machines are each at operating speed, the recordist calls, 'Sound ready,' and the cameraman calls, 'Speed' Somewhere in all this, the First Assistant will shout, 'Quiet please!' Sound stages usually also have a 'Red light and Bell' system that warns everyone a take is in progress.

The camera operator usually says, 'Mark it.' The most junior assistant holds up the clapper-board in front of the camera and says, 'Slate [or Shot] 76, Take 1.' The assistant then smartly raps the top of the clapper-board down on the lower part so that there is a point visible on the picture corresponding exactly to a point on the sound track and removes the clapper-board. The camera operator then indicates that the camera is ready. Then either the director will call, 'Action!' or the First Assistant will call, perhaps using a walkie-talkie to cue people out of range of normal voice contact.

At the end of the take, the director calls, 'Cut,' and everything stops. If all is well and the gate is clean, the First Assistant shouts (they only get the job if they like shouting), 'That's clean everybody, moving on!' (or something of the sort). If there is a problem, we go for another take, still of the same 'shot' or piece of action.

Everybody on the unit knows exactly what is going on and there is no room for misunderstandings.

Traditionally, the director stays by a film camera and watches the action from there. Over the past twenty-five years there has been an increasing use of 'video assist', which means the director can see what the camera is seeing during the take. It is also usually possible these days to listen, through headphones, to the sound as it is recorded. This is useful, because the highly directional microphones we often use may not pick up noises that seem loud in real life, and other noises may sound much louder through the microphones. The director can hear exactly how big the problems are. Getting the sound right is harder than it looks!

Videotape

Videotape is a long plastic strip coated in metal oxide. The tape is not light-sensitive but is sensitive to magnetic fields. In an electronic camera, the light image is converted into an electrical signal that may be stored on such tape. The principles are the same in a camcorder costing a couple of hundred pounds and in the latest Digi-beta widescreen camera costing twenty or thirty thousand pounds. It is all a matter of refinement.

Some cameras that you can buy in Comet or Dixon's give pictures that are as almost as good as those we used to get from our best colour cameras a few years ago. They work with tapes that are about the same size as old-fashioned sound cassettes. We can now record pictures digitally, too, onto some form of disk drive.

Why do we use the expensive cameras? Basically because they are far more sensitive than cheaper cameras, there are far more fine adjustments we can make to suit different lighting conditions. At the time of writing, the sound quality on the cheaper cameras is also less good. When we use the sound and the pictures in editing, the processes can get very complicated. The original signal may have to be copied and recopied. On cheap digital systems the sound quality may not be up to all this manipulation.

On the other hand, we do use the cheap, light cameras for really awkward places. It is easier and safer to use a domestic digital recorder, for instance, to get shots from a moving car window without complicated camera rigs. I also used a very small camera like those you can see in the High Street stores for a shot on *The Demon Headmaster*. I wanted to see the point of view from a tiny camera built into a 'green hand badge' as the badge was picked up and pinned to an actor's jacket. A camera the size of the badge would be impossibly expensive for us to build, but the domestic camera was light enough and small enough to give me the shots I wanted. I do not think there are film cameras that could do the same job so easily or cheaply. There are also slightly more sophisticated, more robust versions of these 'domestic' cameras for professional use.

The tapes are cheaper and longer than rolls of film. The usual tape length on location that I have come across is 30 minutes. The biggest problem with tape is that there are so many formats in use across the world. Not only are there different types of tape, the way the picture may be recorded varies from one country to another. The conversion of pictures from one system to another is improving all the time, but it is still not perfect.

There is a lot of talk about the digital revolution. Widescreen televisions have become available and there are plenty of programmes being shot in widescreen. So far as the actor is concerned, this should usually be irrelevant. The director and camera operator will tell you whether you are in shot and what your marks are – and that is all the actor really needs to know. The different formats available in video cameras and tape should not affect the essence of the actor's work.

Phrases to do with videotape and going for a take

I think it is fair to say that working with a video camera tends to be just a little less formal than working on film. As we go for a take, you may hear, 'Run to record,' or 'Turn over.' There will usually be a slightly longer run-up than on film. The sound recordist may have a sound tape running in parallel to the camera, but we normally use the sound that is recorded on the videotape. Again, the camera operator will call, 'Speed.' The First Assistant will shout out the shot (or slate) number and the take, and then it will be time to shout, 'Action' Often, video-camera crews do not bother with a clapper-board. Sometimes they do not bother to shout out the slate and take number. The reason is that professional video cameras record a time-code with every frame of the picture. When we review or edit, we can choose to see or to hide the time-code.

If we are using a cheaper, lightweight camera, it is likely that we will also record sound on a separate machine to improve the sound quality. If this is the case, we may also use a clapper-board to provide a picture and sound synchronisation point. You may see some crews using a clapper-board anyway – it can make it a little easier to find different takes at the edit.

At the end of the take, if all seems well, you may hear, 'Cut' or 'Stop and check,' which means stop recording and make sure we

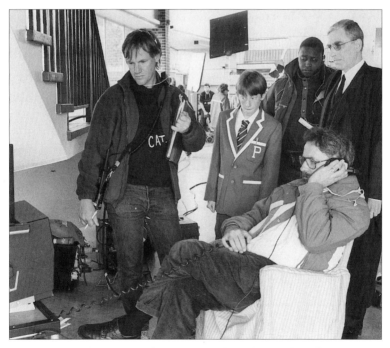

Playback – checking a recording on location observed by members of the cast.

recorded something. If all is well, then someone will call, 'That's clear', Then we move on.

As with video assist, there is usually a monitor available for the director to watch the recording. One of the advantages of a video system is that it is possible to watch a playback of the shot that has just been recorded on the director's monitor. This explains why the director sometimes disappears from sight during a take – what we do not want is a crowd of people looking over our shoulders at what is going on. It can be very distracting.

Video cameras do not suffer from hairs in the gate or scratches. The metal oxide may occasionally fall off the tape in places and this can spoil the picture. If it happens, it is called 'dropout' and it means doing a retake. Modern digital cameras are so clever that they can compensate for quite a lot of tape damage whilst still delivering a brilliant picture.

SOUND

Although it is possible to use a boom on a single-camera shoot, it is much more common to use fishing rods (which may sometimes simply be called 'poles') and radio mikes. The sound assistants on drama shoots tend to develop a very strong pair of arms because of the length of time they have to hold the poles over their heads.

Out of doors, the mikes will be protected by a large cover called a windshield. This will be covered again by a furry grey 'sock', which cuts out most of the sound from the wind.

We quite often have to do a retake because of a sound problem. The commonest is 'Plane!' If we have more than one shot in a scene and there is the sound of a plane passing (or any other type of vehicle), we will have a problem at the edit, sticking the two shots together. The sound of the plane would come and go every time we changed the shot. It is possible to add more plane noise to even everything out, but often it has to be so loud, it drowns the dialogue. Anyway, that would not work for any period piece set before the invention of jet planes! This kind of problem can affect any kind of shoot, film or video, not just drama.

The day begins

How the day begins depends on where we are recording. Many locations and film studios are difficult to get to by public transport. If the journey time would be excessive for the children taking part, the production will have to organise hotels for them. If it is not practical for the chaperone to collect her charges in person, and if a parent cannot drop off the child at a convenient place, then the production should provide transport. Sometimes, children travel to their stage school where a coach picks them up. The production is responsible for the children door to door.

There is no particular reason why a unit has to begin work at 9.00 a.m. It can be earlier. Children, though, should not be working before that time if they are under 13, or before 8.30 a.m. if they are between 13 and 16 (unless there are exceptional circumstance that have been agreed with the local education authority). Nonetheless, I have come across individuals who were called, as under 16s, as early as 6.00 a.m. More common would be a pick-up time of 7.00 a.m. Others have begun proper work well before 8.30 a.m., apparently on a regular basis.

I am not suggesting that these infringements of the law (for that is what some of these were) have done any harm to the children affected. Clearly, though, where abuses do take place, there is the possibility that children's welfare may suffer. Companies that allow these infringements are also gaining an unfair advantage over those that don't – their schedules can be shorter, and their charges lower or their profit higher.

If the scenes for the day are being shot on a film stage, breakfast is no big deal. It may make as much sense to eat at home or in the hotel, as at the studio restaurant. The fun begins on location.

It is usual to bring all the children working on a particular day to the location in time to be ready for rehearsal at nine o'clock in the morning. Although there is great pressure to cut costs on all programmes, it can be a false economy not to have location catering.

Location catering

Location caterers turn up in a van. They provide hot breakfasts and lunches as well as hot and cold running tea, almost on demand. Even a small unit can generate thirty mouths to feed, and it is not difficult to top one hundred!

In the morning, there will a wide choice of breakfast. The wagon with its tiny built-in kitchen provides a range of food that can include anything from sausages to kippers. Any of these can be squeezed into a roll, on demand. Lunch provides a choice of starter and main dishes; these days at least one of these is likely to be vegetarian. There will also be a range of salads and puddings, as well as more tea, coffee and juice. A lot of these caterers pride themselves on the afternoon tea, too. Even hungry children will not starve.

'What if it rains?' I hear you ask. We may make arrangements to use a village hall or to build a marquee, if there is no suitable room. If all else fails, we bring in a dining bus. This can be a single- or double-decker bus converted so that seats face each other across tables, as some do on Inter-City trains. Between meals, if there is no other suitable place, the tutor will use a dining bus as a classroom.

The standards of catering do vary, but I have always found that children new to the business are impressed with the range, quantity and quality of the food available.

OTHER FACILITIES

If we cannot have access to a suitable hall, and if the location itself cannot provide washing and lavatory facilities, we bring those in, too.

Obviously, if we are using a family's house as a location, we cannot descend on them with the entire location unit. Sometimes, the caterer and the support vehicles may need to be a little distance from the location itself. In this case, we may have to provide a minibus to ferry everyone around. The support vehicles may include a costume and make-up caravan, sound and camera cars, a prop van for the furniture and props we will need each week and perhaps a van for a carpenter and painter with their tools and materials.

Overall, it can be quite a circus. The drive now is to work with smaller units at reduced costs. It took a long time for people like Anna Home* to raise the profile of Children's Drama so it could attract the sort of budgets that would let us work as quickly, flexibly and professionally as an adult-drama crew, and provide us with the facilities they would expect. There is no reason why a children's drama should cost less than an adult drama and, because of the restrictions on children's hours, there are reasons why it should cost more. If children's drama is worth doing, it is worth doing well.

---

* Anna was the BBC Executive Producer, who brought *Grange Hill* to the BBC, gave me my first job as a director and became Head of BBC Children's Programmes. There is a lot more I could say about her part in starting TVS and her work for the EBU and other international organisations influencing Children's Television across the world.

Costume and make-up

As with the studio, the first stage of preparation is to change, then to make up. There will rarely be individual dressing rooms on a location. Film studios may have this luxury and high-cost feature films may have caravans for the stars. A typical costume and make-up caravan may have three make-up places with chairs and mirrors, enough space for a changing cubicle, all the costumes, a washing machine and an ironing board. It is usually possible to arrange mains electricity and a water supply.

If we are in one place for a long time, it is sometimes better to transfer all the costumes and equipment to suitable rooms at or near the location. If we have to move from one place to another every two or three days, it is much easier to use the caravan.

Apart from the different surroundings, the whole make-up and costume process is very similar to that of the studio. The main difference tends to be that the make-up and costume teams are more wrapped up to keep out the cold.

Rain can be a problem, too. It is a funny thing about rain. It can be raining quite heavily before it shows up on the camera. (If we have

Keeping the cast dry – on location
with *The Lion, the Witch and the Wardrobe*

to shoot a rain sequence, we usually bring in a rain effect.) This means that we can keep shooting even if it is wet. We may not be able to see the rain, but it is certain we can all feel it and as certain that hair, wigs and costumes will soon start to drip. So Costume are well provided with umbrellas to keep the actors dry. The crew, of course, not being seen, can be muffled up in thermals and waterproofs.

A WORD ABOUT TEMPERATURE

There are some people in a film or television unit who work hard physically, who are always dashing around. For many, though, including the actors, there can be a lot of hanging around. We try not to waste time, but there are always last-minute adjustments to the set, to costume, to make-up or to the lights that are not long enough to send actors away to do something else.

Now, it is a funny thing about scripts and units. The writers often have in mind a time of year, like the Summer Holidays (especially for children's drama). We may try to shoot in the summer holidays, because the days are long and there is no need to worry about tuition but we often find ourselves working out of doors in the winter. Even if we are working at a supposedly warmer time of year, we can still end up being snowed on in April. It also happens that we start a scene on one location on a nice warm day and have to follow it up at a

A cold moment on location –
Frances Amey as Dinah Hunter in *The Demon Headmaster*.

different location on a wet and chilly day – it is the same day in the story but the shooting of the scenes may be weeks apart. So any actor may be asked to wear summer clothes on a day when thermals would be a good idea (and vice versa).

What with the hanging about and clothes that are wrong for the actual weather, it is easy for any actor to get cold. Children tend to be smaller than adults and they can lose heat more quickly. For rehearsals and in pauses, therefore, the dressers may throw a coat round the child actors' shoulders. One costume designer I know carried adult-sized Puffa style jackets for this purpose. They were so big and so different from the proper costume, that we could not begin a take without everyone noticing if one of the coats had not been removed.

If you are a child actor, and you are offered such a coat, it is for a reason. We do not want you to be chilled and therefore vulnerable to coughs, colds or other bugs. It is not a fashion show, and no-one is going to think you are anything less than sensible for keeping warm!

Rehearsal

I try to have a couple of days of rehearsal before going on location. I find that anything we have looked at in rehearsal goes better on location. The actors and I remember a lot, even if we change everything and have only sketched in a rough plan of a scene.

Frequently, there will be no rehearsal apart from the read-through. Sometimes there may not even be that. You get to location and someone, maybe the director, says, 'Hi, this is Fred [Bill or Joe]: he's playing your father [brother, uncle, boyfriend].' And you have to get on with the first scene of the day as though this total stranger is someone very important in your life. What is more, the way you play the first scene has to harmonise with the way you play every other scene. It is easy for an inexperienced adult actor to start playing a character one way but to end up wishing he or she had started playing it with a different emphasis. For children, it is up to the director to stop problems like this from arising.

I try not to start on the first day of shooting with the first scene of the project. On the first day, everyone is getting to know everyone else and the ways of working. Sometimes, we try and start with a light day – a few necessary but straightforward scenes. It is good to end the first day comfortably on schedule – and even to make a start on the next day's work. Of course, this is not always possible.

What I will do is to rehearse the entire scene – not just the first shot – so everyone can see the shape of the work in hand. Over breakfast, I will already have talked to the Lighting Director or Lighting Cameraman about the first scene, precisely where the actors will be and how I plan to shoot it. By the start of rehearsal, the lighting crew is already at work, moving lights and cables into position. The Sound Recordist and assistant are setting up their equipment out of the way of the first shot. As soon as it is safe to bring in the actors, we start working out the scene. On location, actors have to rely heavily on the director. It will usually be clear where a scene has to be. It will be clear if people have to enter and exit. There is a lot that follows from the shape of the location, so we do not start with an entirely blank canvas.

Some directors work with storyboards. These are sketches of key moments in each shot, which show how each scene is to be shot and edited. Everything is decided beforehand, although the actual interpretation of lines, mood and expression will still come from the actor. At the other extreme are the directors who make it up as they go along, writing nothing down. Of course, there are times when all directors need to use a storyboard. It is hard to do effects sequences

On location – child actors in *The Demon Headmaster*
listen to the director.

without them, and they are useful, too, in planning dangerous-looking stunts.

My system is to provide a sketch with a floor plan showing where the actors and the camera are in relation to the setting. I also list the shots I would like. I regard this as a statement of intent, not as something totally fixed. As I direct the actors through the moves I have planned, there is room for them to say if something feels wrong or unnatural. We work through the scene, talking about possibilities for each line, so that we may put across to the audience, not just the meaning of the words in each line, but some other emotion the characters may be feeling or thoughts they may be thinking. This is all part of what is meant by 'sub-text'.

Sometimes, we also talk about motivation. This is something that adult actors consider a great deal. It is not something that bothers most child actors. I say, 'OK you walk into the kitchen and find your sister there.'

An adult might say, 'Why am I walking into the kitchen?'

It is the director's job to understand the question and to provide an answer better than, 'Because it says so in the script.'

Helpful answers might be, depending on the rest of the plot, 'You have just got back from the game of football in Scene 212, and you are going to put your muddy gear in the washing machine, then you are going to get a cold drink. You are surprised to see your sister home so early.' Or, 'You have just found the clue to the buried treasure you have both been searching for. She has just come in through the back door and you can't wait to tell her the news.'

I think you will see that the way you go into the kitchen would be different with these different thoughts in mind.

While we are rehearsing, the camera team will be watching and may suggest better shots than I have planned. They will also want to look at the positions of the actors to make sure they can see them in the shot as I hope to see them and to make sure they are lit properly.

It can take all morning to shoot a long scene, or all day if it is a very long one. It may be a sunny day, and the sun will move round, changing the way shadows look in the kitchen (the effect can be even stronger outside). It is not just a matter of pointing the camera and shooting – the lighting director will be planning the look of the whole scene and will also be thinking about other scenes in the story. Because we have discussed the scene before the actors arrive on the set, we will have decided on the best way to start shooting. 'Best' also takes into account what is likely to be straightforward for the actors. The next chapter should make this clearer.

13 *Still on Location – Shooting*

We have reached the point where we all know what is going to happen in the whole scene. The designer has time to check the background and the production team has made sure everything else is ready – all the right props are in place, ready and safe.

How do we shoot a scene with lots of shots and only one camera? There is no simple answer. All kinds of things may affect how we decide to shoot any particular scene: there may be reasons to start in the middle, or to start with a particular actor's lines. In general, the simplest thing with a short scene is to shoot a 'master shot' and then go in for detail.

A sample scene

A 'master' may cover the whole scene or only a part. It may be sensible to record a master for the first two pages of the scene, then another for the next two, and a third for the last three pages. There is no general rule. Every person on the unit – including the actors – has to be flexible. However, I will take a simple example, of the boy entering the kitchen to find his sister. The first shot would be the master. It might be framed to show Sister in the foreground making herself a sandwich. It would make sense to see in the background the door that Brother is to use.

I have rehearsed the actors; the next thing is to rehearse for camera and sound. The actors walk through the scene slowly, going to their correct positions: Brother joins Sister at the work-surface. Sister crosses to the 'fridge and puts the butter away. She turns to face Brother. They talk. They agree to go out and look for the rest of the gang. Sister leads the way out through the same door Brother has used and, pausing only to grab an apple, Brother follows. The running time for all this is, say, a couple of minutes.

The camera operator needs to check the focus for Sister, then for Brother when he stops by her, as she turns away from the camera to look at him. The focus needs changing again as Sister crosses to the 'fridge and turns to face Brother (and the camera). Then we need to ensure that the shot is still focused as Brother reaches to the foreground bag of apples and hurries off through the door. We say, as these adjustments are made, that the camera operator or assistant is 'pulling focus'. Meanwhile, the sound assistant is holding the fishing rod mike high over the camera, keeping the mike angled towards whichever character is speaking and moving it to follow the action.

While all this going on, there will be time taken to check the focus and to tell the sound assistant that the mike has just dipped into shot on a particular line. There may be a mike shadow on the wall behind Sister when she has finished putting the butter away. If there is, there will now be a pause to sort out the problem. Maybe the sound assistant will have to stand somewhere else. (This could be difficult in a cramped kitchen full of a tv unit.) A light may have to be moved to get rid of the shadow.

At last, all the problems are solved and we shoot the 'master'. Sometimes, we manage in one take. It can take more. In fact, with a master shot, it may be the case that I am fairly certain that I am going to use it at the start of the scene, for the move to the 'fridge in the middle and for the apple-grabbing and exit at the end. It will not matter too much if there is some blemish of performance or technical skill in some other part of the shot.

Retakes

If the shot is 'clean' and I am happy with the performances, we move on. Otherwise, we do a retake.

In a scene like the one in a kitchen, I would not necessarily expect the camera to move. There may, however, be problems with keeping everyone nicely in shot, or 'pulling focus' so that everything you want to stay sharp is sharp, moment by moment.

Of course, things can get much more complicated. Tracking shots can look great. This is where we put the camera on a dolly, which can run either on track or on a very smooth floor. If two or three people are walking along, chatting, it makes sense to stay with them and to use a track. For the actors, it means saying the lines properly, walking at a consistent pace and keeping an agreed distance from the other actor(s). If everything works, it is great, but there are more things to go wrong. If the pace is too fast, we run out of track and the dolly may jolt off the end of the track. If any of the actors sway a little too much whilst walking, they may go out of frame. It may be harder for the sound assistant to keep the microphone in a good position to pick up the dialogue and so on.

One of the things I talk about to child actors new to location work is the kind of problem we meet when tracking. Not everyone finds it easy to get right. I have had to resort to putting one highly intelligent but scatty child between two others better able to cope with walking in a straight line.

One of the problems working out of doors is the light. The sun moves. One part of a garden in the background of the first shot of the day may be in deep, deep shadow. An hour later that area is flooded in sunlight. Lighting continuity can be difficult. Clouds can also cause problems. We start a scene in cloudy conditions. The clouds break up. Two awkward things may happen. One is that the sun comes out halfway through a take. The eye can cope but the camera cannot. The other is that we have a scene half-shot in nice even lighting under cloud, and the rest in the sharp contrasts of bright sunlight. It takes time and patience to overcome these things.

One way to cut down on performance retakes is to arrange for the difficult or complicated scenes to be shot early in the day when everyone is fresh. At the end of a long day, fatigue can begin to show. Even an experienced adult may find the going difficult, with an increasing number of retakes.

There is great pressure to save time (and money) and not do retakes. Much can be done at the edit to get round slight errors and generally to turn 'sow's ear' scenes into 'silk purses'. One problem with groups of child actors acting together in a scene is that some need more rehearsal than others. If I go for a take too early, some performances won't be at their best. If I go later, then other children will have gone 'off the boil'. It can be a hard judgement. Generally, I try and favour the child with the most difficult part in that scene.

This leads on to the question about what happens if actors – especially child actors – think they could have done a particular scene, or shot, better. Actors do say this to me. With adults, if there is time, I will generally try and do another take unless I know I can get over the problem in editing.

With children, I will usually have a clear idea about how the finished scene will look, and expect the child to trust my judgement, because going again might not improve matters. If I do not think the child has got the most out of a line or a scene, I will ask for another take. The difference is that a good adult actor can vary a performance with great subtlety and will have clear thoughts about exactly what to do differently – many child actors are a little more erratic.

Often, too, the reason for another take may be a thought that the actor (or the director) has only just had – we don't have long for rehearsal. Sometimes, there is nothing specific that is wrong with a scene. It just needs a 'brisker delivery'. Sometimes I remind young actors to make their lines sound as though they've only just thought of them – that is often the case when we have been working on a scene for a long time, and everything is beginning to sound 'learnt'.

The scene continues

In our sample scene, the next logical shot will be to shoot Brother's lines when he first comes in. You may hear the terms MS, MCU and CU. These mean: 'Mid-Shot', showing someone roughly to the waist; 'Medium Close-Up', showing head and shoulders and 'Close-Up', showing only the head and neck. In the example I am describing, changing from the 2-shot* to any of these is fairly straightforward. The lights stay more or less static, and so will the camera. We can shoot the whole of Brother's move and the lines. This will mean a quick re-rehearsal so the camera operator can check focus and the sound assistant can check where the mike needs to be.

We shoot that shot. If there is a fluff (where the actor says the wrong word, or forgets a word, or the word comes out the wrong way), we may go again from the top (beginning) of the scene. If the first few lines are OK, we can do a 'pick-up'. This means we go back a line or two before the mistake, and pick the scene up in the middle. We keep on going until we have a good performance on all Brother's lines from this angle.

If there is a particularly important line or phrase, we can do that bit of the script again, in an even closer shot.

The biggest single change, the one that usually takes most time between shooting one shot and the next, is moving the lights and equipment. The less that has to be moved, the quicker the move will be. In my example, the next shot is as Sister puts the butter away and turns to face Brother.

Once that shot, and all the rest, are 'in the can' (which referred in the first place to an exposed reel of film in its lightproof tin box), it is

---

* A 2-, 3- or 4-shot is one showing 2, 3 or 4 actors. A shot showing more than 4 or 5 actors is a group shot.

Costume drama
– on location for *The Phoenix and the Carpet*

be time to turn everything round to look the other way. This will let us see Sister's face as Brother talks to her for the first part of the dialogue. This shot would even work with Sister crossing to the 'fridge. After this, I shoot Brother's shot as the conversation continues after the butter has been put away. I might even have a close shot of the paper bag with the apple being taken, if the apple were important.

The shots

So, we have a straightforward scene with two actors, not doing anything very complicated. I suggest that we would need at least the following shots (the sketch plan, drawn exactly as I would if this were a real scene, may help make things clearer).

1 The master with all the action.
2 Close on Brother for the first part of his dialogue (I shall ignore the possibility of a CU on Brother).
3 Close on Sister for the second part of her dialogue.

Then there would be the big move.

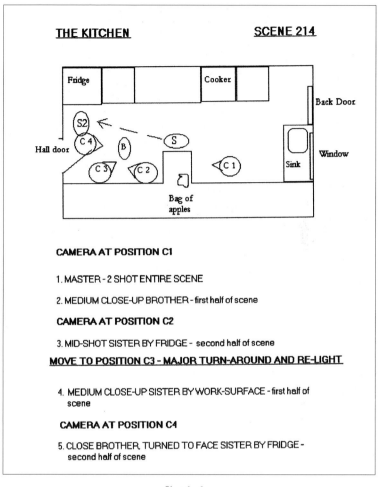

Sketch plan

4 Close on Sister for the FIRST part of her dialogue.
5 Close on Brother for the second part of HIS dialogue.

You will see, I think, that we have covered the scene completely several times and that we have not stuck simply to the story order. I would expect the whole scene from starting rehearsal to moving to the next scene to take about a couple of hours.

Of course, we might find a way of making the whole scene work within just one slate (or shot). In a confined space like a kitchen, it is sometimes difficult making the action look natural with both faces visible at once. In real life, most people prefer to face each other when they are talking. It is not often natural to get two people to have an intense conversation when they are both looking in the same direction.

With a small number of people in a scene, it is usually quicker to shoot all the dialogue than to set up and record each line separately. The flow will be better, and I often find that moments when characters are listening can be as dramatic as moments when they are speaking. A shot where someone is not speaking but is listening, or looking at something else, is called a 'reaction shot'. In a scene like this, I would take reactions from the material I have listed.

Of course, if there is a long scene and someone has only a couple of lines in the whole thing, then I might shoot just those lines with a little bit on each side from the other actors.

Because we sometimes have to work in confined spaces, we sometimes have to 'cheat' positions. Looking at the sketch plan, it is clear that the camera operator has not got much room with the camera in position 4, and Sister might well have to squash herself into the corner to make room. Brother might also have to 'cheat' himself back a bit, closer to the Sister's first position.

Just how the scene fits together at the edit is difficult to describe. I would probably use each angle more than once, so there might be more than a dozen changes of shot in the scene from the five slates and four positions.

More difficult scenes

Obviously, it can all get very complicated. I may have to change the order of shooting to release a child, because it is getting to the end of her day or because we have to make up tuition time. Everything can get more complicated out of doors, or with more actors in a scene, or with 'action' sequences (like fights), or with animals, or with special effects.

I can give three examples of the sorts of problem that can arise on location, all of which called for patience and understanding from cast and crew. In the third series of *The Demon Headmaster*, the villain ended up in hospital. The Executive Producer wanted us to use an air ambulance – a helicopter. Any helicopter shot is expensive, and to hire a helicopter and kit it out to look like an air ambulance would have been far too expensive. Instead, for a contribution to funds, we

Period exteriors – a corner of a Victorian street
in *The Phoenix and the Carpet*

were able to get the Virgin London Air Ambulance for a couple of hours. Of course, we knew that if there were an emergency call, it would fly off and we would never see it again. It seemed worth the risk but, because of this possibility, I decided to take all the helicopter shots as soon as the helicopter arrived. This meant shooting the middle of the scene, then the end, as the helicopter took off and flew away, then the beginning which showed two characters arriving in the middle of the excitement. Even I was confused – but we got some great shots.

On another occasion, in 1981, I was directing *The Story of the Treasure Seekers* in a version that generally stuck closely to the book. The Bastable family begins by digging for treasure in their back garden. They are joined by Albert-next-door, who is something of a wimp. He gets buried in the treasure tunnel when it collapses. To make this safe, we used a special effect made by BBC Visual Effects. We were shooting in Tunbridge Wells, in Kent. The Visual Effects Designer, Peter, made the hole at the BBC Visual Effects Workshop in West London, put it in the back of his car and brought it to Tunbridge Wells. Once there, he took the hole out of his car and put it in the garden. This took time. When it came to it, the effect only half worked, so the hole only half-collapsed. (It was an interesting hole made of wood.)

The trouble with effects like this is that they are mostly one-offs. They always work in the workshops, but there may be unforeseen problems on location. It is important that everything is safe. The actors need particular concentration and they need to be aware that these effects are expensive and difficult to build. There may only be one chance to get it right – especially with things like fires and explosions. A lapse of attention can spoil a morning's work and waste an afternoon in setting everything up again.

In *The Story of the Treasure Seekers*, we had a location scene where the cast had to play a Victorian game. The scene began with a picnic. Then the sound recordist said, 'I can hear an electric drill.' Electric drills had not been invented when the story was written. My First Assistant (Production Manager) ran off, looking for the phantom driller. Then I noticed a bee on the tree under which we were filming. Then I noticed another bee. The tree was large. It was in full blossom. It was covered in bees. THEY were source of the 'electric drill' noise. We could not ask them to go away, so WE had to move to another part of the garden and begin the scene again.

Mention of the differences in sound between shots in the same sequence brings me on to the next issue.

Continuity

This is a big topic. I have made two tapes about it that together run for an hour and I have written a book about it, too.

In a multi-camera set-up, we try to record scenes or sequences in one go. The actors act the entire scene, and it is up to the camera and technical crew to make sure everything is recorded properly and that we see what we need to.

In a kitchen scene like the one just described (in all single-camera scenes, really, except 'one-shot wonders'*), the action would be broken down over the two hours of shooting time. Later, with the editor, we would put all the bits and pieces together to make the action look as though it had really all happened in two minutes.

To make it convincing, there must be continuity from shot to

---

* 'One-shot wonders' was the name I first heard on the second series of *Grange Hill*. We used that term for shots that (as you might expect) covered an entire scene in one shot. Often, this would be when we had fallen behind schedule on an earlier scene and needed to do something to catch up. The real trick is to make the scene work so that it does not look as though you have done it that way just to save time.

shot. I always have someone looking after continuity on my drama programmes. In the BBC, the production assistant has usually done this job. On all three series of *The Demon Headmaster*, my production assistant was Alison Leon. Sometimes on films and increasingly on tv Drama productions, you see credits for Script Supervisor or even just Continuity. These people would be doing what Alison was doing on my series.

Alison's main job on location was to watch the action like a hawk. She had to notice – and note down certain things.

- What the actors were wearing.
- How clothes were worn (e.g. how many buttons, if any, were done up on a coat).
- What each character did.
- When each action started – that is on which line of dialogue.
- Which props were in shot and how they were arranged.
- How the action changed the props.

And much, much more.

To help in this impossible-sounding job, she used a Polaroid camera to get a record of how each scene started and finished. The costume and make-up designers had their Polaroid snaps of the actors, too.

In our kitchen scene, Alison would have noted what sort of sandwich Sister was making; what order she put the sandwich together; when in this process Brother arrived; what brother was carrying – and in which hand it was – and where he put it down; at which line Sister moved towards the 'fridge; which hand she used to pick up the butter; which hand she used to open the 'fridge door; which shelf she put the butter on (which would affect how far Sister had to bend down) and so on.

Sounds difficult? It is.

One of the virtues of a good actor is to be consistent. As the rehearsal goes on, the moves fall into place with the actions. Actor and director between them should be able to make the script work to tell the story. The actor learns the moves with the words. Once rehearsal is over and we have shot the master, we refer everything back to that.

If Sister picks up the butter in her left hand on the master, then she should do the same on all her other shots – even if we cannot see the butter. Her left shoulder will move if her left hand goes towards the butter. If she uses her right hand on the mid-shot, then we would have to do a retake and Alison would have a quiet word with the actor to remind her about this bit of continuity. And of course, if there has been a gap for relighting and moving equipment, the actor may ask for a reminder about which hand to use.

I have emphasized continuity because it does make everything work and look right. If Fred is in the shop wearing a red tee-shirt and he walks out into the street on the next shot wearing a blue tee-shirt, some of the audience will see at once what the problem is. Others will notice that something is wrong and use part of their minds for working out what. Either way, the thread of concentration is disturbed. We have lost the audience. There are enough distractions to watching a television drama without our making mistakes like that!

14 Being on Location – Trials and Tribulations

On a cold wet day, when you are soaked through and fed up with all the technical problems, when you have been shooting one long, difficult scene with effects and animals and crowds, and when the cameras seem to have shot every line from every possible angle, you may wonder why anybody wants to be an actor.

On the other hand, it is mostly quite a good feeling, telling a good story, working as part of a team and getting paid for it.

A lot of what I have written in the last three chapters is as true for adult actors as it is for child actors. I find myself giving a note to a mature adult actor and turning to the novice 10-year-old to give another note in just the same way. Obviously, for each I will try and give a note that will make sense – but in that scene the child and the adult are both necessary, both important. Without either, there would be no scene. For once, the 10-year-old is treated in an adult way, as an equal.

This is a two-way process. I expect child actors to take even a comedy seriously. It is important that no-one wastes time by being late, by forgetting to learn their lines, by forgetting to check in their schedules what scenes we have today or simply by not paying attention.

The last three paragraphs apply equally to multi-camera studio productions.

Costume and make-up – odd problems

Shooting on location can be slow. It may not be energetic. At lunchtime, then, what is more natural than to work off the excess energy with a little football? Well, the problem is that people playing football get hot and sweaty. This can be a surprisingly big problem – apart from the danger of getting costumes muddy. If you play football for half an hour in the sun, you are liable to become very flushed –

157

maybe even a little sunburnt. I have known it take the make-up artists half an hour to get a group of boys back to looking as they did before lunch. We lost time we could ill afford.

Clearly, costume is important to a drama. Even if the costume is a sweatshirt and a pair of jeans almost like those the actor would usually wear, they need to be separate and to be looked after. The Costume Designer has to make sure everything is ready for each scene when it is needed, in the state it needs to be in. If the character in the story has been playing football, then it might be right for the jeans to be muddy. Sometimes, there might be two sets of some costumes, allowing a scene with muddy jeans to be shot before a scene where the jeans are clean.

It can happen that one costume needs to be worn over a number of days to complete a sequence set on one story day. Working with the Costume Designer, we usually have a couple of dressers. It is their job to help the actors get the costume as it should be – to match the continuity of the story. The washing machine on the Costume caravan will help the dressers keep clothes clean and fresh for the actors to wear. 'Clean' dirt, sweat and rain spots can be added if necessary.

Looking right is important to actors. It is therefore important for them to take reasonable care of their costumes. Don't spill custard down them. Don't play football in them. Don't leave them lying around on the set or off it. On the set, if you take off an item of clothing, hand it to your dresser (or the costume designer). If you are in the changing area, hang it up. If you do, it will make life easier for everyone. Children who do not, rapidly become very unpopular with their dressers and with the costume designer – not to mention the rest of the production team!

Points of view

From programmes like *Auntie's Bloomers* and *It'll be All Right on the Night*, most of you will have seen the sorts of things that can go wrong in the studio and on location. Often, mistakes are funny at the time to us. Less often, they are funny to a wider audience. It can be fun working on location and it can be difficult – it can even be both at the same time. I asked my panel of experts about difficult moments, perhaps being too wet or too cold.

Jim remembered a time when he had been too wet. 'My little brother had to fall in the river in Derbyshire four or five times –

freezing. And he said he was freezing cold. They'd given him a dry-suit but it leaked … I did the one in *999* and my dry-suit leaked straight down my arm.'

Adele commented, 'Kids love doing it and they put up with it. The best thing they ever invented are those hand-warmers. You can put them in your shoes as well. Brilliant.'

With all the talk about rivers and cold, I wondered if any of the young actors had ever felt in danger.

Jim said, 'No, on *999* we had a little demonstration by the divers and they had safety lines and things.'

I have not come across anyone who admitted to feeling in danger. I knew one boy who said he was quite comfortable in a flying harness, six feet off the ground. A few seconds later, he asked to come down and promptly threw up. The operators of the flying equipment said it was probably that the harness had restricted the blood flow in his legs. He was OK again a few minutes later, but it does go to show that it does not pay to try and be stoical or 'macho'.

Lauren commented, 'If they give you things, they have to make sure you know how to work them. Like when I was abseiling, they went really over the top to make sure I was OK.'

If they'd felt safe, I wondered if any of them had felt exploited. Adele's response was quick, 'Pampered!'

Adele was speaking as a young actress with a main part. It can vary. If there are crowd scenes with fifty or more 'background artists', there is bound to be some sense of feeling like part of a herd. And some background artists (among the adults) do sometimes abuse the system – I have heard caterers complain of some individuals getting away with up to three helpings of a main lunch course.

I have offered 'walk-on' work to children in the past as some kind of consolation prize for not getting a big part. I wondered if the young actors felt this could teach anything. Adele again had a response. 'If you do it, it gives you an image of what it'll be like [to act].' But she clearly felt that there is a big difference. Certainly it can be tedious, being a background artist. I think there is a workload that is challenging and satisfying. If it is exceeded, it becomes exhausting; if it is not reached, boredom may breed frustration.

For a child actor, things do change from one production to another as the 'child' matures. Gunnar Cauthery says, 'I find that as I get older and I am increasingly aware of the subconscious processes behind what remains an instinctual art form, my attitude improves on set and I feel more at ease with myself off set than I did as a naïve

13-year old ... I did experience some distress when filming the first series of *The Demon Headmaster* because I became Lloyd Hunter for seven weeks and ... was shocked by some of my actions, which were uncharacteristically volatile ... [However] when I worked on *Just William*, later that year ... I was calmer, more focused and better prepared to undertake my rôle.'

A word from the director

I have tried to give an impression of what happens on location. Each child will experience it differently. I enjoy directing, building up a story from the script with the actors and crew. It is a team effort, and the image of myself as the conductor of the orchestra – dependent entirely on each member of that orchestra to perform each function with great skill – constantly occurs to me. I find the work challenging and satisfying. I enjoy working in the studio and on location.

There are, of course, moments when we have had more than enough retakes for passing planes and scudding clouds; when the special bit of equipment that means we can look at a computer screen has not arrived; when the tripod has just fallen over and smashed the camera; when the leading boy has just had a row with the leading girl. Then, we all wonder about getting some other more predictable job.

There are other reasons for unhappiness on a project, too. One boy felt exploited by a particular production. When filming a weekly children's show once every six weeks at the rate of three shows a day for two days, they had to get, effectively, an hour in the can per day. On a drama, in a multi-camera studio, I would think we were doing well to record over twenty minutes – less with children.

It was, he says, a highly intense and often unpleasant experience. With that schedule, there was no margin for error at all. He usually worked for about seven to eight hours per day with breaks, but no tuition. The pressure was to get everything right first time, every time. He was unhappy with the results and invariably fell asleep in the taxi on his way home. I know the series he means. The children quite often had to do very silly and, in my view, demeaning things.

On the other hand, doing something as well as you can, with other people who are all working with you, and, after a good mornings's work, relaxing at lunchtime in the shade of the trees whilst enjoying location catering, make up for all that. It can be very hard work for us all – but it can be fun, too. There are children who do not seem to have a great deal of talent or aptitude, but I have not come across any children who had good parts who regretted the experience.

It is because the whole system depends on teamwork that I would agree with Anna Scher that it is unhelpful to talk about 'child stars'. Child actors are a vital part of the team, but there is no guarantee that they are going to want – or to be able – to carry on with acting all their lives. After the shoot, they must go back to school. But more of that in the next chapter.

Postscript – post-production – post-synching – pre-recording

After the shoot is over, the director (usually) has to work with the post-production team to put everything together. An editor puts the pictures and soundtrack together. Sometimes there is specially composed music, which means working closely with a composer. Sometimes there are lots of trick effects, which may mean working for some days with a Video or Digital Effects Designer. The Dubbing Mixer fine-tunes the sound and adds sound effects and music. It is usually only at the dubbing stage that actors may be required.

In a post-synching session, we might call in one or more actors to say some lines again that have been a problem on the original shoot. This may mean saying the words again exactly as they were said on location, matching the new words to the original mouth movements. This is time-consuming and requires considerable concentration, but is not much more difficult than, say, singing in unison. A simpler variation on this is where an actor's voice is needed to add commentary or 'inner thoughts'.

There are two more thoughts about sound. One is that songs may be pre-recorded in a sound studio for playback on location. On location, the actors may then have to sing in synch with their pre-recorded voices. This is much easier than trying to record a song line by line. Again, the trick is to think in terms of singing in unison.

The whole post-production process may take weeks, and it is a time I usually enjoy because the good bits of the shoot get better and the awkward bits become respectable. Apart from post-synching, the actors are not involved. Important though this stage is, I do not think it is necessary to say more about it here.

15 *After the Shoot is over*

So, it is all finished. The child actor has used up all forty or eighty days allowed, so there is no more acting for a while. What is left? Is it worth it? And would you still want to be a child actor?

Glamour – or not?

I wonder what satisfaction child actors get from acting. It seems to me that some like the applause, the fame. For others I think there would be satisfaction in helping make something – in telling a good story. Not many have Thomas Szekeres's experience of going to the première of Kenneth Branagh's (and William Shakespeare's) *Hamlet*, complete with a string quartet and champagne.

Some, like Rachael Goodyer, find our end-of-shoot parties and programme viewing quite glamorous. 'And,' says Rachael, 'having your own driver is something I always boast about to my friends.' Several others like this, too.

Seb admitted enjoying being recognised as he walked down the street, even though it could be a bit embarrassing at times. Most of the young actors seem to half-like the recognition – who would not? – but it can be hard to deal with. Gunnar tells of one particular bad experience. 'I had been on a coach for about sixteen hours and hadn't slept at all. I was eating breakfast on a ferry, when suddenly a group of very boisterous young girls collected round the table and asked me to autograph their arms! I also find that a surprisingly large number of people get a kick out of being deliberately rude to someone they recognise from television.'

Adele said, 'I don't really tell anyone. It's always my friends who tell. There's a woman I know who tells the whole street. And then when I go round to see her, it's, "This is the one that's in *This or This*." Or, "Have you met HIM? Ooh, get his autograph."'

'Someone I know was going on, saying, "Oh, are you going to see your show-biz mates?" And it's not like that. It's people doing a job

… They're doing something they love and, at the end of the day, you know them for who they are. I don't think there is anything glamorous about it. It's just another job and it's fun. It's a really good job to do.'

When she was doing a pantomime, Lauren found that she got more of a buzz from her friends saying, 'Well done!' than from the actual applause.

On the other hand, Lucas had worked for a time on *Les Misérables* in the West End. Several times, there had been a standing ovation. When he'd used up all his available performance days, on his last night, there was no such response. Lucas demonstrated, by flicking the fingers of each hand upwards, how he had rather cheekily 'asked' for a standing ovation. 'All of a sudden, people started getting up. It was like a Mexican Wave. I wasn't expecting this. "Jean" [the main character in the musical] pushed me forward to take a bow myself because it was my last night. And as I bowed, it was just incredible – the buzz! As soon as I came off it, I thought, "I'm never going to be on this stage again!"' Lucas said all this made him feel tearful.

I wondered – not for the first time – whether there is much danger of children getting swelled heads. One deterrent to big-headedness for some is the fact that they do not like seeing themselves on television. Adele is one of those who watch self-critically and think how to get it better next time. I do that myself – if you don't think you can do better, then maybe it's time to try doing something else! Seb agreed, 'You're always critical of it.'

Highs and lows?

Adele is really a 'young adult' actress, not a 'child'. When I asked about the highs of acting, she said, 'Getting to know people, being able to discuss the scene you're acting in; getting some feedback from the other actors as to what they think the scene meant.' She also admitted that it was good to talk to the director about these things, too! Several people mentioned 'getting to know people' as one of the pleasures of acting.

I got a far better response when I asked about the lows. Adele kicked off. 'You get a bad day – lots of takes.'

Jim agreed, 'Yes, lots of takes. When you know everyone's getting irritated. If you can't get something right, whether it's reacting, acting or something physical … I had to fall off a car once and it took something ridiculous like twenty-five takes. They wanted to do it a certain way because I wasn't actually falling off the car – I was falling onto a little mat. They wanted me to look a certain way and get the timing right.'

Adele understood this – and that doing lots of takes, for lots of shots from different angles, gets worse if you have lines to say. 'You've done a scene that many times, your mind starts going blank – you start forgetting.' She remembered one particular scene that had seemed quite brief and straightforward. The director chose to cover it from a lot of angles, so that meant the two actors had to perform the scene several times. Then there were retakes for all sorts of reasons, like traffic noise.

'By the end of it, ... we couldn't remember exactly what we were supposed to say because we were completely worn out. That was a really bad day ... It was only a tiny scene and they never actually put it in, in the end!'

For Frances Amey, the downside to acting on location is the early start that we make. She sent me a very expressive drawing showing the 'big bags' under her eyes!

Rachael Goodyer did not want to be too specific. 'All I will say is that it is always difficult to get along with people you live with every day, on set and off set. There will be arguments between cast members. Try and avoid them – but you'll always make up.'

The money

Two or three child actors pointed out that children don't have to earn a living, unlike adults. One boy said, 'I don't do it just for the money. Even if they'd paid me half as much as I got, I'd still do it. I don't have to make a living to support me – I've still got parents. Obviously, when you get older, you need to go your own way and start to earn your own money.'

There are families in this country where the child's income from acting or advertising is significant to the family resources. For children at stage school, part of the money earned will go to the agent as commission and some may go to help pay school fees. (Of course, agents do generally take commission, even where the children do not go to full-time stage schools.) It is a very uncertain business, as much for children as for adults. It is not wise to rely on such income. The family that used the money to pay for the daughter's interest in music was, perhaps, wise. It is true that some children start well and continue well: Jodie Foster began as a young child advertising a sun lotion. She is now a highly successful movie star. Her brother also acted as a child but ran into career problems as he was growing up. Success is not guaranteed.

Ian Smith at the Children's Television Workshop in Nottingham also has words of caution. 'I think maybe the danger comes with the amount of money a child can earn and the attitude they may then have towards earning money in the future … Maybe approaching acting for the wrong reasons – seeing it as an earner rather than something which they're passionately involved in? That would be my main worry.'

Surviving success

Grange Hill was successful and has survived into its third decade. When the first series began in 1978, the world of television was different. There were only three channels and home computers were still just in the future. It was possible for the BBC to claim an audience of ten million for its new Children's Drama, which became a rival in popularity to Blue Peter. Some years later, *The Demon Headmaster* scored five million viewers or thereabouts for the run of its first series in 1995 and was, I believe, the top-rated children series of the year. Now, two-and-a-half to three million viewers would be a highly respectable score. It is not likely that any other children's drama will make the sustained impact of *Grange Hill* (in the early years) or that a child acting in such a series will have quite the same problems that this caused.

I spoke to George Armstrong who played Alan Humphries in the first few series of *Grange Hill* and its sequel, *Tucker's Luck*. His views and experiences are interesting.

George followed his older brother, Adam, to the Italia Conti Academy. At the beginning, he did not have any great ambitions to be an actor. He certainly did not believe that he had star quality.

With *Grange Hill*, George became very well known. His character, with Benny, played by Terry Sue Patt, was part of the programme's principal trio headed by Tucker (Todd Carty). Fame brought its problems and George says that if he knew then what he knows now, '… I'd have done it differently. Becoming that well known changed us drastically.'

For the first two years, he enjoyed the recognition but, 'At 15, we weren't mentally prepared for the life that went with [this fame]. We weren't worldly wise enough.' He feels that it would have been easier to cope if he'd been older.

By 17, it was becoming difficult to handle. In many ways, he feels he 'lost his youth'. Everywhere he went, he was recognised. He felt that he was always being watched. If he or his fellow actors had done anything untoward, it would have been meat and drink to the newspapers.

On a date, he would wonder whether the girl he was with wanted to be with him or was interested in him only because of his part on television. Also, when he did go out, he was not allowed to give his attention to his companion because there would be constant interruptions from people who had recognised him.

It took him until he was 20 and was finishing the last series of *Tucker's Luck* to reach the conclusion that, 'This was the life I'd chosen – I'd got to accept it.'

He works now with an actor's co-operative agency as an actor, and as a theatre lighting designer at a school near Brighton. The second job involves him in coaching and advising on various aspects of theatre work. On *Grange Hill*, he learnt about acting on a television set. Theory is one thing, but '… it's the learning curve, being there, that makes you know about it.' Even to this, he adds a caution, 'At 15, you think you know it all and you know nothing!'

It is since he left Alan Humphries behind him that his love of theatre has grown. It is theatre that has taken him to work in Australia and London as well as Brighton. Looking back, much has changed. More places now teach actors television techniques. You are more likely to find courses that cover the technical aspects of film, tv and theatre. George says, 'The more you know [about the technical aspects] the more it helps you as a performer.'

He warns, though, of the pains of acting. 'It is the most heart-rending business in the world.' He gave as a tough example going to an audition for an advert and being turned away almost straight away '… "because you don't look right." You need rhinoceros hide.'

He thinks of the child actors who began with him in *Grange Hill*. Few are still acting. One runs a wedding dress design business; another is a housewife in Scotland. Those who are still acting, like Terry Sue Patt, have parallel interests such as writing. One or two, like Michelle Gayle (who was starting as George was leaving *Grange Hill*), have gone into the entertainment side of the business as singers.

On the other hand, both George and I have worked, separately, with David Parfitt, another former child actor who was one of the producers of *Shakespeare in Love*!

George said, 'I'd have liked to be more detached – not so much in people's faces.' He agreed that a shorter involvement with the series might have eased some of the problems. Certainly, now, he would be wary about becoming a long-running character in any other series.

On the other hand, child acting gave him a nice start in life. George has been able to pay his own way since he was 14. He had sound financial advice from his father about investments and even pension schemes, so he has always had something 'for a rainy day'.

I asked George if he would encourage a child of his own to go to stage school and beyond. He said that stage school had helped him to become confident and outgoing, and he thought such opportunities might be beneficial for others. As for going on to acting as an adult, '… whether I'd like a child of mine to act or perform – I'm not convinced.'

Viewings

I know that there is a sense of let-down at the end of each production. I think that is why most shows try and throw some sort of end-of-production party, where all the cast and crew are invited. It marks the finish, gives an opportunity for us to say 'thank you' to everyone, gives everyone a chance to say goodbye (or *au revoir*), and to exchange phone numbers.

Sometimes, it is possible to lay on a viewing for cast and crew, too. This will be weeks later when everything has been finished. This is good fun. It is a good reunion and the tiredness that can be with us on the last day of production is absent. It is odd that all the weeks – or months – of effort can be condensed into a viewing time of perhaps three hours. At least with a serial of six parts (or more) the transmissions take several weeks. It is not a case of, 'Blink and you've missed it.'

Street and school

As George Armstrong found, it is not always easy to cope with instant recognition. The reaction of school friends can be surprising. Popularity and congratulations are easily coped with. Some resent such success and are jealous. Whatever the cause, there can be at least a few unkind remarks from schoolfellows. Rachael Goodyer says that, 'Those who give negative reactions aren't worth thinking about and I always block them out because I know for every bad reaction there are ten good ones.'

It can happen that members of school staff join in with unpleasant remarks, too. 'You needn't think that just because you're a television star you're ... going to get away with not doing your homework!' Teachers need to be careful what they say. It is easy for a 12-year-old to misunderstand heavy-handed adult banter and to be hurt. Of course, deliberate verbal bullying is even worse.

Gunnar says, 'What I was totally unprepared for was the reaction from school friends. I found that people I had never spoken to before would greet me as if we had known each other closely for years, while others were extremely hostile, and quite merciless in their ribbing. I would attribute this to the green-eyed monster ... What was also distressing was that the odd teacher at school would behave in a cynical or unpleasant way towards me without any reason, as if to say, "Oh, look at him, isn't he the big-time luvvie?" or some such phrase.' He adds, 'I always welcome constructive criticism or advice because other people can see things I may not notice about my performance, no matter how self-analytical I am.'

I have heard, too, of physical bullying and assault, and not just in school. Most people are friendly and interested, but it has happened that a child actor has been approached in the street with, 'Hey, aren't you the kid on tv last night?' 'Yes.' Bang – a smack in the face.

I do always warn children that they should be prepared for bad reactions.

Tom Brodie played Sean in my series *Watt on Earth*. It was not all plain sailing for him. 'I often got picked on because I was 'famous'. The name of the programmes didn't help ... as comments such as "What on earth are you doing here?" did get a bit annoying ... I became very modest and sometimes denied it was me in the programme.'

It can be tough on young actors who play 'hard' rôles. There was a racist bully called 'Gripper Stebson' in a couple of series of *Grange Hill*. It was said that the young actor who played the part – in reality a very nice lad – had had a difficult time with boys who wanted to 'take on' Gripper. These bullies appeared to have been unable to see the difference between the character and the actor.

I had asked everyone I contacted whether the attention made child actors big-headed. Tom's reply – especially following on from his last comments – is typical. 'I was more proud of my achievement than big-headed, but the pride was soon quashed by the ribbing I would get at school.'

I asked Kristy Bruce what would cure her if she ever did get a swelled head. Her reply was brief and to the point: 'My sister!!!'

On the other hand

It is quite usual for there to be a press launch of a new season on a major network. With the BBC, there has been at least one (and more recently two) per year, just for Children's Programmes. When this happens, leading actors from the drama series are invited along to meet the press and to see a video promoting the new season's works. Like the appearances of some child actors on CBBC and CITV, this means giving sensible answers to questions that may not be particularly sensible. These occasions are to help make people aware that the series or the project is coming on – it is a form of advertising for the production. We sometimes get journalists on teenage papers coming along to recordings to cover the backstage story, too. It is all to help us get more people watching.

One of only two glamorous occasions that Gunnar can call to mind was just such a press launch. (The other was the première of a film he made in Iceland.) He was part of *The Demon Headmaster* contingent. 'On that occasion, I met a large number of people whom I recognised from television, including Zoë Ball, a poster of whom was on my bedroom wall at the time, and who actually approached me and introduced herself.'

Maybe he was lucky. You can sit all through one of these events without anyone famous or even any reporter coming anywhere near you!

Of course, Children's Programmes are more likely to put child characters centre stage than productions for adults, so children are less likely to be involved in the publicity for 'peak viewing' programmes.

Is it worth it?

No child actors I have met wished they had not done it. Lots try it and go another way as adults. Some children, like Frances Amey, began as child actors and now wonder whether they wish to continue to be professional adult actors. Some, like Rachael Goodyer, have completely different careers in mind, but want to continue performing in some form or other while they can.

I don't think that not getting parts as a child will stop someone with both talent and determination from becoming an actor. Drama classes can help confidence and development, but this is also true for those who learn to play a musical instrument – and this has been demonstrated scientifically.

Simply wanting to act is not enough. The line you hear in many tv programmes and films that runs something like, 'If you want it hard enough, it'll happen,' is just not true. Equally, if you don't want it hard enough, it won't happen. As someone has said before, 'It's a hard knock life'.

If I knew then ...

I asked people for tips about work as a child actor. I got a wide variety of responses from the kind of advice Anna Scher and other adults give to their students through to thoughts from child actors along the lines of, 'If I knew then what I know now ...'

Advice from adults

Anna Scher

Anna has written a book called *Desperate to Act*. It may be possible to get hold of library copies, but it does not appear to be in print now. In our interview, she said, 'I would say that, definitely, the child should have a second string to their bow ... I was desperate to act and my [grandfather] said, "Over my dead body! You do something socially useful like be a teacher. No way will you act!"

'We came to a compromise. I was going to go to a teacher training college, get properly qualified ... so I'd have my passport to security, so to speak. He was absolutely right and I will be eternally appreciative for that advice. I've passed that baton on to a lot of people.'

Her advice for children was this: 'You must have training. If there isn't a drama centre near you, perhaps you can cajole your drama teacher to run some sort of drama club. See as much theatre as possible and films. Write your own reviews. Read literature and drama. "Reading is to the mind what exercise is to the body."*

* Sir Richard Steele in *The Tatler*, 18 March 1710

Anna summed up her message to parents, 'Don't take away their dream, but just make sure there's a second string to the bow.'

Stage schools

I asked Mr Vote at Italia Conti's what he'd say to parents who said their child was a performer, to a parent who was pushing. 'It isn't their decision,' he replied. 'It's their child's decision. I think it should be made on the basis of advice received from professionals in the business. Teachers can see talent. In any group you work with, a talented child stands out a mile. If a teacher approaches you, then you can begin to think about it. Then you've got grounds to think about this kind of training.'

He also noted the difficulties and sacrifices some children faced to get to the school. 'Many travel long distances or stay in town during the week. The price of doing this is that you lose contact with your friends. If that's very important to you, then you really should not be thinking of a specialist school.' He pointed out that Conti's is a small school, and that there is not the range of fellow-students to make it easy to find that special friend – although, he added, 'There can be advantages in going to a smaller school.'

The Sylvia Young School and its agencies, Young 'uns and Rossmore (for over 16s), in Marylebone, has been very successful since it opened in 1981. They have so many people writing to them for advice that they have a standard letter of advice running to five pages. I shall quote just a part of it:

'If you are unable to consider or obtain a place at a stage school or theatre school, you should look for part-time schools in your area. Many theatres have excellent youth theatre groups. Check with your local library or council newspaper for information.

'Go to the theatre as often as you can. See as many straight plays as you can as well as musicals. Go regularly to your local theatre and if possible go to the Royal National Theatre, the Royal Shakespeare Company and West End theatres.

'Although there are advantages to attending a theatre school at a young age, we always recommend further training from 16 years. There are many options for courses in the media at local colleges. We feel that this should be followed by aiming to get into one of the main drama schools from the age of 18. Places at these drama schools are very limited. There is so much competition – and there may be diffi-culties in obtaining grants, but try – if you are serious about becoming a professional actor you should do a 3-year course at an accredited drama school.

'We even recommend the students who attend our full-time school to go to drama school at 18.'

There are many courses available now in Media Studies. There are currently more students and graduates of these courses than people working in our industry. Media Studies as a subject is not something that will necessarily help anyone get into show business. This is not what most of these courses are for. There are university courses in drama, communications studies and other topics that may well be helpful. Take any advice you can on the courses you think might be relevant.

There are of course some successful actors who have not been to a drama school. It does not suit everybody. You can read more about becoming an adult actor in Nigel Rideout's book, *First Steps towards an Acting Career*.

Junior Television Workshops

Ian Smith offers this comment: 'I would be concerned if a parent was reading this book and saying, "I want my child to act." Because that says to me, "That's about YOU wanting to act."

'I think if you are encouraging your child towards that, you have to examine your own motives very, very strongly and be careful that it isn't you who wants to act and you're living vicariously through your child.'

It was Ian who made me aware of the range of and number of members of the National Association of Youth Theatres. He thoroughly recommends support for that movement, especially in view of the threats that he sees to drama in the school curriculum. 'If your school offers drama, then make sure you take as much advantage of it as possible … Seek out places where young people are doing good drama … I think there is a bad drama experience that you can unwittingly subject your kids to. One can get into a sort of situation run by well-meaning old biddies who are throwing dusty old things at the kids.' He warns of the dangers of originality, honesty and truthfulness in a child's approach to drama being 'bashed out of them' by poor teaching methods.

Ian also talks with enthusiasm of the benefits of drama – in school and out of it – to the children who cannot read this book and cannot communicate their interests and emotions, but who need to do drama and to benefit from the experiences of telling a story or exploring another character's world.

He believes strongly in regionality. For him, it is important that children keep their own accents. He advises that RP is useful as an accent. 'It is the most important second accent, I suppose.'

I can see the value of drama as a subject at school and wish it had been one of my options.

Stagecoach

Stephanie Manuel, the founder of Stagecoach, says, 'I always say to my kids, "Actors need to be educated, just like everybody else."' For her, drama is an important part of education. Many Stagecoach students have got professional work, but this is perhaps less of an object for Stagecoach than for the full-time stage schools – or even for the Junior Television Workshops.

Thoughts from a director

Any actor could do worse than to remember the Scout motto –
BE PREPARED

FOR AUDITIONS

Make sure you know the time of the appointment, who the contact is and the exact address where the auditions are being held – it is not necessarily at the headquarters of the Production Company! Try to get as much information as possible from the agent about the nature of the part or about the project. For instance, if the audition is for an advertisement, it will help you to know something about the product to be advertised!

Children are likely to be asked what they've done. I also often ask who the director was on a particular project. Questions like these are common, and it does not take much to think of a sensible answer! I can understand someone not remembering the director's name if the actor was very young and was only there as part of a crowd, but I think any speaking part should give enough contact with the director for the first name, at least, to be remembered.

Some productions may ask for photographs. If you are expected to turn up with photographs, I think the agent should know that and warn you. I don't ask for them; we usually aim to take Polaroid pictures of all the children we see.

Try and turn up in good time. Try and avoid turning up with the whole family. Reception areas get crowded very quickly.

Try and enjoy the audition. The casting people can't eat you – and they want to see you at your best. Anyway, they may be almost as nervous as you are!

If you go for a recall, do not deliberately change your appearance. (Obviously, you might be in school uniform on one occasion and not on the other, but you could avoid having, say, a drastic haircut!)

Do not be thrown by the way other people play a line or a part – unless you are told something specific about the meaning of the line, or a way to play it, do it the way that seems natural to you.

If you get the part, well and good, but don't let it go to your head. You saw how many other people nearly got the part. If your licence is refused (and this happened to a boy I wanted on *The Demon Headmaster*), the fact is that there is someone else who will be able to step into 'your' part and do very well with it. This is why allowing your head to swell is never justified.

If you don't get the part, don't worry, you may get something else. If you never seem to get a part, it may just be the luck of the draw – but you may feel it is worth asking yourself whether there are other aspects to television that you would find almost as much fun as acting.

SHOOTING

Be there in good time – or be ready to be collected in good time.

Make sure you have your script and your schedule with you. Make sure you know each day what you are supposed to be doing.

Do focus your mind on schooling during tuition periods. The shoot lasts a few weeks at most. You have the whole of the rest of your life to live!

Do listen to the director, the First Assistant and whoever is looking after actors.

Do listen to your chaperone.

If you feel unwell, tell your chaperone or parent, but be prepared to keep going if you reasonably can (that is without endangering yourself).

If you are unhappy, under too much pressure, if anyone is really upsetting you or, heaven forbid, bullying you, tell your chaperone or parent, or even your contact on the production team.

BUT be prepared for the frictions you would expect from day to day with any group of people you spend a lot of time with.

Finally, do LEARN YOUR LINES.

THE END OF THE SHOOT

Don't be surprised at the feeling of deflation or anti-climax. This is quite common.

Don't be surprised to be recognised in the street: don't be surprised if nobody appears to have seen your performance.

Don't be surprised if some people think you were great and some thought you were terrible. You (I hope) did your best and as the director wanted.

Don't be surprised if you get no more offers of work or if you get loads. Whether it was successful or not, whether you enjoyed it or not, it was an experience you can learn from.

Don't forget that at 8, 10, 12 or 15 – even at 21 – you may want to be an actor. Three years later, you may want to change your mind. Don't close doors on yourself!

Advice from child (or ex-child) actors

Charlotte said, 'Don't give up – there's always another school if you don't get your first choice.'

George said, 'It's hard to get into stage school: don't get your hopes built up.'

Daniel said, 'Use your initiative – don't rely on everyone else.'

Caroline said, 'There is luck as well as talent.'

Nicola said, 'Never think you're too good for a small job. Someone might see you on that and give you something else. You're never better than anyone.'

Adele's advice is, 'Relax and enjoy yourself.'

Seb added, 'Yeah, pick it up as you go along.'

Jim thought that giving general tips was very difficult. He would be happier to comment on specific things about each part, but no two parts are quite the same. (Nor are two production teams!)

Child actors I have directed

Thomas Szekeres, 'Always go for the banoffee pie over any other dessert and don't let what other people say to you get to you. Don't be reluctant to say something "strange": it is the character, not you.

'If you work hard, keep your feet on the ground and aim high.'

Rachael Goodyer says, 'What I always do is write down my lines for the day in my schedule so you can recap just before you go on set. If you're prepared to do all the hard work (and there is a lot of hard work) then go for it!'

Tom Brodie says, 'If you treat every job as your last, you will never be disappointed. This attitude is good to have early on.' He also thinks it would be helpful to have a family member who was a casting director or agent ...

Kristy Bruce says simply, 'Be careful of jealous people!'

Gunnar Cauthery says 'I wish I had known beforehand how to deal with the attention and how to avoid being consumed by one's own rôle, but these are the sorts of things which I could never have hoped to understand until I went through them, and I would go through everything again, without hesitation.'

He feels show business is not something to be entered into without careful consideration, but that if you take care and think things through, '... it can be magic.'

Useful addresses

I have deliberately not included agents and stage schools in this list because there are so many.

Contacts is published in October by *Spotlight*

Spotlight is published by
The Spotlight
7 Leicester Place
London WC2H 7BP
e-mail: info@spotlight.cd.com

National Association of Youth Theatres
Unit 1304
The Custard Factory
Gibb Street
Digbeth
Birmingham B9 4AA

External examination bodies mentioned in the text

The Guildhall School of Music and Drama
Barbican
London EC2Y 8DT

The London Academy of Music and Dramatic Art
Examinations Department
226 Cromwell Road
London SW5 0SR

Trinity College London (Examinations)
16 Park Crescent
London W1P 4AN

The English Speaking Board
26A Princes Street
Southport
Merseyside
PR8 1EQ

Sources of information – for students and young adults

British Actors' Equity Association
Guild House
Upper St Martin's Lane
London WC2 9EG
(Youth membership possible from age 14–16)

National Council for Drama Training
5 Tavistock Place
LondonWC1H 9SS

ALSO

Contact individual drama schools and universities for the range of courses each offers. There are handbooks listing which universities run which courses. Schools and public libraries should have copies.

The Internet has entries under University Drama Departments and many UK courses are detailed on the Standing Conference of University Drama Departments Links Web Site at: www.ex.ac.uk/drama/links courses. html

Useful sources of information if working in the United States of America

The AFTRA-SAG Young Performers' Handbook
(a joint project of the American Federation of Television and Radio Artists and the Screen Actors' Guild Young Performers Committees)
AFTRA are based at –
260 Madison Avenue
New York
NY 10016
USA

SAG are based at –
5757 Wilshire Boulevard
Los Angeles
CA 90036
USA

Book List

First Steps towards a Career in Acting
by Nigel Rideout, published by A & C Black

Television and Children and *Continuity Notes*
by Roger Singleton-Turner, published by BBC Television Training
(now known as BBC Television Development and Training)

The Job of Acting
by Clive Swift, published by Harrap

Desperate to Act
by Anna Scher (out of print but available in some libraries)

The Law on Performances by Children – a guide to the children (Performances) regulations 1968 and related statutory provisions and the *Children's Act* should be held by your local education authority. Copies should be available from Her Majesty's Stationery Office, London.
Please note that these regulations are being superseded by new Europe-wide legislation. New information should be available from the same sources.

Index